Co

G000162187

CONTENTS

4

Introduction to

Gran Canaria

Basking in gentle subtropical temperatures and year-round sunshine, Gran Canaria might have been custom-designed as a holiday paradise. One of the largest of the Canary Islands and a territory of Spain, the island lies just 210km from the coast of West Africa but 1250km southwest of Cádiz, the nearest point on the European mainland. It's far enough south to have almost guaranteed good weather making it a hugely popular winter destination for northern Europeans.

Most come to enjoy the busy beaches and nightlife, but beyond the resorts there are plenty of secluded coves, colonial towns, volcanic landscapes and beautiful forests to provide an antidote to the urban hedonism.

▲ Playa de Meloneras

When to visit

Weatherwise there's no bad time to visit Gran Canaria. Winter is the mainstay of the island's tourist industry, when daytime temperatures peak in the low 20's Celsius, making sunbathing perfectly viable, though swimming pools are sometimes unheated and subsequently chilly. Christmas and New Year are the peak season, and prices soar accordingly. Las Palmas claims to have the best climate in the world, though sunshine records and peak temperatures are higher in the drier south, while the high hills of the north can be enveloped in cloud at any time of year and snow, though rare, is not unknown. Carnival and Easter are popular times to visit the island, while after April the summer season starts, with prices rather lower than the winter peak, though in August the island can still be very busy. The hottest temperatures are experienced in the late summer and early autumn, when much of the south of the island can appear dry and barren. In contrast, January and February, when the almond trees bloom and the hillsides are green, sees Gran Canaria at its most beautiful.

▲ Temisas

Gran Canaria was first settled around 500 BC by peoples from North Africa who called the island Tamaran. Their culture was largely obliterated by the Spanish conquest in the late fifteenth century, an invasion that they fiercely resisted, but they left behind a rich archeological legacy that's worth exploring. Today's islanders are the descendants of the original Canarios and of the settlers from Spain and other European countries who arrived post-conquest. Fascinating traces remain of this colonial era too, when Las Palmas was a way station on the route to the Americas and the seat of the Canary Islands' bishopric, the royal court and the Inquisition. The island experienced successive agricultural booms based on wine, sugar, cochineal, bananas and tomatoes, but economic downturns caused many Canary Islanders to emigrate to South America and the Hispanic Caribbean. In the nineteenth century the importance of the island as a refuelling port for steamship traffic brought significant investment from British and other foreign merchants.

Lasting prosperity arrived with the tourist boom of the mid-twentieth century, and the island is now stuck with a package tour image. However, while it's true that resorts strongly associated

▲ Puerto Rico

▼ Banana plantations, Arucas

with mass tourism, such as Maspalomas and Playa del Inglés, do have their ugly hotels, cheap beer and all-you-can-eat breakfasts, they also have attractive bungalow complexes set in luxuriant gardens, excellent restaurants and vibrant nightlife.

Away from the resorts, Gran Canaria packs incredible diversity into its 1560 square kilometres, from the cosmopolitan buzz of the capital, Las Palmas, to the sleepy colonial towns of the north and the ruggedly beautiful mountains of the interior. Rural tourism in characterful hotels and self-catering cottages increasingly offers an alternative to the tried-and-tested sun and sand formula, as do the burgeoning golf tourism trade and the island's international reputation for windsurfing. As if all this were not enough, there's a busy schedule of cultural events and fiestas, from opera, Carnival and world music to saints' days and festivals based on the rituals of the original Canarios. No wonder Gran Canaria is often called a continent in miniature.

▼ Playa de las Canteras, Las Palmas

Gran Canaria
AT A GLANCE

Las Palmas

Gran Canaria's exhilarating capital is a tale of two cities: a stately and cultured colonial one with excellent museums and many historic monuments, and a vibrant, cosmopolitan port and resort with one of the world's great urban beaches.

▲ Las Palmas

Telde and the east coast

Cave dwellings and rugged scenery make the beautiful Barranco de Guayadeque a must in the east of the island, while the windsurfing at Pozo Izquierdo is superb and the quiet colonial sections of Telde, Ingenio and Aguïmes are well worth exploring.

◄ Barranco de Guayadeque, Telde

The Cumbre

A World Biosphere Reserve and an open-air lesson in vulcanology, the island's mountainous interior is a paradise for walkers and cyclists, and can also be explored by car or jeep. Roque Nublo is the symbol of the mountains, and from 1949m Pozo de las Nieves you can watch the sun sink into a sea of clouds.

◄ The Cumbre

▲ Playa de Aldea, west coast

The Costa Canaria

From San Agustín to Meloneras a vast and efficient tourist industry has colonized the former tomato fields of the island's sunny south, but at the heart of it all the golden dunes of Maspalomas offer escape, solitude and great natural beauty.

▲ Santa María de Guía, the north

▼ The Costa Canaria

made beaches and the highest sunshine rates on the island. Further west, the landscape is lonely and spectacular, culminating in the unforgettable Andén Verde coastal drive.

The north

From the cool green hillsides above Vega de San Mateo and Valleseco to the luxuriant banana plantations of the coast, the island's north is lush and agriculturally productive, dotted with unspoilt colonial towns and home to much of the island's wine industry.

The southwest and west

The coast west of Meloneras is rocky and rugged, but the resorts of Puerto Rico, Puerto de Mogán and Patalavaca have golden man-

Ideas

The big six

Gran Canaria has amazing diversity as a holiday destination, as its most significant sights prove. They encompass everything from the beauty of the dunes at Maspalomas and the biodiversity of the island's interior to the archeological significance of the Barranco de Guayadeque and the exquisite architecture of Vegueta, Las Palmas' colonial quarter. For a truly memorable travel experience, the scenic thrills of the spectacular Andén Verde drive on the west coast are equalled only by the infectious hedonism of Carnival.

▲ The Dunes of Maspalomas

A mini Sahara at the southern tip of the island and a haven of peace amid the noise and bustle of the resorts.

P.116 ▶ The Costa Canaria

▲ The Cumbre

Just a short distance from the resorts, Gran Canaria's pristine centre is a World Biosphere Reserve with dramatic volcanic scenery.

P.97 ▶ The Cumbre

▶ Carnival

Dance away the blues at Gran Canaria's biggest winter party and make sure you stick around for the Burial of the Sardine.

P.70 ▶ Las Palmas: Ciudad Jardín to La Isleta

▲ The Barranco de Guayadeque

Cave dwellings and the traces of the pre-Hispanic Canarios make this narrow canyon the most memorable valley on the island.

P.89 ▶ The east coast

▼ The Andén Verde

Nearly 30 kilometres of light, sea, scenery and vertigo, the spectacular Andén Verde drive is the highlight of any round-the-island trip.

P.147 ▶ The west coast and the Andén Verde

◀ Vegueta

The most complete colonial city on the island, Las Palmas' old quarter is stately, historic and – after dark – vibrant.

P.51 ▶ Las Palmas: Vegueta and Triana

Six essential Gran Canaria experiences

Sunny weather and sandy beaches are the main reason most people come to Gran Canaria, but if you take time out from the beach to discover the island's other pleasures you'll be rewarded with a range of experiences from the freshest sea fish you'll ever taste to the mysterious relics of the pre-Hispanic past, and from the island's incredibly varied coastline and rugged, unspoilt mountainous interior to its pretty colonial towns.

▲ Discover the island's unspoilt mountainous interior

Trek through pine forests, conquer volcanic peaks or just picnic in the beautiful sur-roundings.

P.97 ▶ The Cumbre

▼ Explore colonial towns

Take a trip back to the island's colonial heyday with a stroll through Aguïmes, Santa Maria de Guía or Teror.

P.156 &P.161 ▶ The north &
P.90 ▶ The east coast

▶ Visit a Canario site

Clamber over the hillsides at Cuatro Puertas or Fortaleza Ansite for a glimpse into the drama and mystery of the pre-Hispanic past.

P.84 ▶ Telde and around & P.97 & P.102 ▶ The Cumbre

◀ Circumnavigate the island

See the incredible scenic diversity of this almost-circular island with a drive around the dramatic and beautiful coastline.

P.145 ▶ The Andén Verde

▶ Eat fresh fish

You'll never eat fresher fish than at a Canarian fish restaurant, often right on the coast with the boats lying only metres away. There are many places you can sample fish, but perhaps the most memorable is Puerto de las Nieves.

P.151 ▶ The west coast and the Andén Verde

◀ Tan on a southern beach

Blue skies, balmy temperatures, soft sand and nothing to do but relax – what are you waiting for?

P.115 ▶ The Costa Canaria & P.136 ▶ The southwest coast

Gran Canaria after dark

Gran Canaria's nightlife cranks into action long after sunset. In Las Palmas, the choice is between the vibrant but sometimes seedy north of the city or the trendy scene in Vegueta and Triana. In Playa del Inglés, the glitziest bars and clubs have international connections and a cool vibe, while elsewhere in the resorts scores of tourist bars cater to specifically German, British, Irish or Scandinavian customers. Drag cabarets deliver resolutely British, end-of-the-pier entertainment, while the island's casinos offer a plush setting in which to place your bets.

▲ Drag cabaret in Playa del Inglés or Puerto Rico

Show tunes, sequins and outrageously funny innuendo Canarian style.

P.129 ▶ The Costa Canaria &
P.143 ▶ The southwest coast

▲ Pacha, Playa del Inglés

Get into the latin spirit of salsa in the stylish surroundings of this upmarket *terraza*.

P.128 ▶ The Costa Canaria

▲ Calle La Pelota, Vegueta, Las Palmas

From café bars to cool DJ lounges, this street near the cathedral is the hottest area in Las Palmas after dark.

P.64 ▶ Las Palmas: Vegueta and Triana

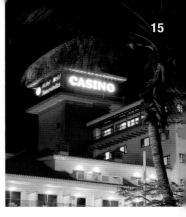

▲ Casino Gran Canaria, San Agustín

Dress to impress and try your luck with the cards or at the roulette wheel.

P.115 ▶ The Costa Canaria

▼ Salsa in Las Palmas

Get the latin spirit with a trip to one of the capital's buzzing Cuban clubs.

P.79 ▶ Las Palmas: Ciudad Jardín to La Isleta

▲ Chinawhite, Playa del Inglés

With great music, beautiful people and a cool vibe this place proves there's more to the south's nightlife than just cheap beer.

P.128 ▶ The Costa Canaria

Souvenir shopping

Stick to the more reputable stores and you'll find a good selection of fashion and sports- or beachwear across Gran Canaria. For souvenirs, check out the high quality crafts from Fedac, the Museum of Rocks at Ingenio or the pottery at La Atalaya. Alternatively, indulge yourself in the luxury stores of Triana or in El Corte Inglés' amazing food hall, where you're sure to pick up a gourmet treat to take home. In the south, Faro 2 remains the nicest of the shopping centres despite newer competition.

▲ Pottery from La Atalaya

Take home a piece of traditional Canarian pottery from this artisan pottery up in the hills.

P.164 ▸ The north

▲ Handicrafts at the Fedac store, Playa del Inglés

The quality is assured and the selection wide at this Government-backed crafts store.

P.125 ▸ The Costa Canaria

◀ Faro II, Maspalomas

The most distinctive shopping complex in the south, selling stylish sportswear and designer fashions.

▶ Lace at the Museum of Rocks, Ingenio

Ignore the machine-made tablecloths and go for the real thing: expensive, but beautiful.

◀ The food hall at El Corte Inglés, Las Palmas

A feast for the eyes and a good place to find tasty gifts to take home.

▶ Triana district, Las Palmas

From local wines to Cuban cigars or designer jewellery, Triana is the place if you prefer your shops small but select.

Cafés and bars

Gran Canaria has a lively bar and café culture similar to that of mainland Spain, with everything from *chocolaterías* dishing up the traditional breakfast of hot chocolate with *churros* to outdoor *terrazas* that stay busy from morning until late at night, serving up hot and cold drinks, tapas and light meals. The boundary between bar and café is somewhat blurred, so that even the most basic bar may have at least a few tapas to nibble with your drink. More cosmopolitan touches include the imported tradition of coffee and cakes, observed in the German-influenced southern resorts.

▲ Café Wien, Playa del Inglés

Have a delicious slice of *Mitteleuropa* at this terrific *konditorei* – and don't forget the whipped cream.

P.125 ▶ The Costa Canaria

▲ Bar of the Hotel Madrid, Las Palmas

Have a drink in this historic gin joint and you'll feel like an extra from a Bogart movie.

P.57 ▶ Las Palmas: Vegueta and Triana

▼ La Parada, Puerto Rico

Right by the taxi stand this simple stand-up bar and café is open for business any time of the day or night.

P.141 ▶ The southwest coast

▲ Terrazas of the Parque Santa Catalina, Las Palmas

Play chess, eat a *bocadillo* or just watch the world go by in Las Palmas' favourite square.

P.78 ▶ Las Palmas: Ciudad Jardín to La Isleta

▼ The café in the Parque San Telmo, Las Palmas

Beautiful *modernismo* architecture and tables under the trees make this a perfect spot for doing nothing.

P.58 ▶ Las Palmas: Vegueta and Triana

▼ El Viento, Pozo Izquierdo

Top spot for windsurfing fans, even the toilets here have sea views.

P.95 ▶ The east coast

Romantic Gran Canaria

Forget the raucous package tour image: there are plenty of peaceful, beautiful places for a romantic break. Small, often highly characterful *casas rurales* in the mountains and villages offer ideal accommodation for couples wanting to get away from it all, and there are stunning sunsets over the mountains and ocean to enjoy together. Even in the busiest places, a barefoot walk along the shoreline or a meal or concert at the ocean's edge is all that it takes to set the scene.

▲ Casas rurales

Rent a blissful hideaway deep in the Gran Canarian countryside.

P.172 ▸ Essentials

▶ Lunch at La Marinera

Bag a window seat at this restaurant on Playa de las Canteras beach and enjoy the ocean views while you eat.

P.77 ▶ Las Palmas: Ciudad Jardin to La Isleta

◀ A concert at the Auditorio Alfredo Kraus

Top-notch classical talent and the stunning seafront setting make for a glamorous night out.

P.79 ▶ Las Palmas: Ciudad Jardín to La Isleta

▼ Sunset at the Montaña de Arucas

Watch the sun sink slowly behind Tenerife from this mountaintop lovers' retreat.

P.159 ▶ The north

▲ A walk along the shore to the Faro de Maspalomas

After a long day at the beach, dip your toes in the water once more and walk hand in hand to the lighthouse.

P.117 ▶ The Costa Canaria

Hotels

There's no shortage of accommodation options on the island for those who prize character and are looking for something a little more distinctive than the efficient but soulless concrete blocks. With everything from peaceful rural haciendas to grand old palace hotels and the developers' latest extravagant fantasy worlds, there's no need to settle for anything humdrum.

▲ Hotel Santa Catalina, Las Palmas

A real grand hotel and still the choice for many VIPs. If you can't afford a suite, take tea on the terrace at least.

P.75 ▸ Las Palmas: Ciudad Jardín to La Isleta

▼ Gran Hotel Costa Meloneras, Maspalomas

A touch of Florida comes to Gran Canaria at this big, stylish resort hotel.

P.121 ▸ The Costa Canaria

▼ La Hacienda del Buen Suceso, Arucas

The perfect holiday hideaway, tucked down a bougainvillea-lined lane and surrounded by luxuriant banana plantations.

P.165 ▸ The north

▲ Gloria Palace, Amadores

Pamper yourself with the thalassotherapy treatments and admire the stunning views at this dramatically sited clifftop spa hotel.

P.140 ▸ The southwest coast

▼ Hotel Rural Las Calas, Vega de San Mateo

Luxuriant gardens, spacious rooms and delicious farmhouse breakfasts make this a real rustic charmer.

P.165 ▸ The north

◄ Las Tirajanas, San Bartolomé de Tirajana

The views are breathtaking at this comfortable modern hotel up in the mountains.

P.110 ▸ The Cumbre

Restaurants

Good eating and drinking in Gran Canaria begins with the local cuisine, strongly influenced by Spanish cooking but with its own traditions too, based on local produce, fresh fish and the use of aromatic *mojo* sauces. Some of the most memorable meals can also be the simplest, in some fishermen's co-operative with the boats pulled up on the beach in front of you. International cooking on the island often means the ubiquitous steakhouse, but highly sophisticated fusion cooking in hip, modern surroundings is also on offer.

▲ Tagoror, Barranco de Guayadeque

Canarian cuisine in a classic Gran Canarian setting – a cave at the top of the Barranco de Guayadeque.

P.96 ▶ The east coast

▲ Casa Montesdeoca, Las Palmas

The romantic setting on the patio of a historic house in Vegueta is memorable, and so is the ice cream with *gofio* and *bienmesabe*.

P.62 ▶ Las Palmas: Vegueta and Triana

▶ La Cava Triana, Las Palmas

The robust flavours of the tapas are perfect accompaniments to the riojas at this casually elegant Triana wine bar.

P.62 ▸ Las Palmas: Vegueta and Triana

◀ El Puertillo, Arucas

Excellent fish and a view of the boats that caught it make *El Puertillo* a good choice for any fresh fish lover.

P.166 ▸ The north

▶ Mundo, Playa del Inglés

Metropolitan sophistication in both the food and the decor make this inventive restaurant a hit with visitors and stylish locals alike.

P.127 ▸ The Costa Canaria

◀ Casa Enrique, Mogán

Take your phrasebook to decipher the blackboard specials at this wonderful Canarian restaurant in rural Mogán.

P.142 ▸ The southwest coast

Food and drink

Salty little wrinkled potatoes – *papas arrugadas* – served with spicy red *mojo* sauce are the one Canarian speciality almost all visitors sample at some stage. The island's staple is *gofio*, a toasted cereal flour used in all kinds of ways, most enjoyably in the thick, fishy *gofio escaldado* soup and in ice cream, or with *bienmesabe*, a delicious mixture of honey and almonds. Farmhouse cheeses, local wines or a bottle of the excellent Arehucas rum all make splendid and inexpensive souvenirs, too.

▲ Canarian wine

Famous in Shakespeare's day, Canarian wine is making a comeback and Gran Canaria has two *denominaciones de origen*, Gran Canaria and Monte Lentiscal.

P.164 ▶ The north

▼ Arehucas rum

Visit the distillery and be sure to try the product – delicious golden Arehucas rum is a reminder that Gran Canaria was once a major sugar producer.

P.160 ▶ The north

▶ Fresh fish

The ocean around Gran Canaria teems with tuna, marlin and swordfish – but don't ignore the less familiar local varieties such as *cherne, vieja* or mero.

P.149 ▶ The west coast and the Andén Verde

◀ Queso de Flor

The queen of Gran Canaria's cheeses hails from Santa Maria de Guía in the north

P.157 ▶ The north

▶ Gofio escaldado

This hearty fish-based soup is served with red onions, mint and a dash of green *mojo* sauce.

P.185 ▶ Language

◀ Mojo

Whether it's spicy red *mojo picón* with *papas arrugadas*, green *mojo verde* with fish or the less common garlicky white sauce, you'll be sure to want to take a bottle home.

P.185 ▶ Language

Folklore and festivals

Beneath the veneer of modern international tourism many of the island's traditions continue unchanged – some celebrating saints' days and others marking more mysterious, pre-Hispanic traditions. Carnival is celebrated in style throughout the island, but above all in Las Palmas, where for a few weeks each year the capital goes *carnaval*-crazy.

▲ Carnival

Mad costumes, elaborate stage sets and sheer enthusiasm make Carnival a memorable experience, from Las Palmas to Maspalomas – but stick around for the Burial of the Sardine.

P.70 ▶ Las Palmas: Ciudad Jardín to La Isleta

▼ Fiesta of the Virgen del Pino, Teror

The island's largest religious festival celebrates the saint's day of the Virgin of the Pine in early September.

P.178 ▸ The north

▼ Folk dancing at the Pueblo Canario

Every Sunday morning in the Pueblo Canario in Las Palmas, you can witness the traditional folk dances of the island.

P.65 ▸ Las Palmas: Ciudad Jardín to La Isleta

▲ Fiestas del Carmen

The fishermen of the island celebrate their saint's day in July, when the fishing fleet from Arguineguín sails to Puerto de Mogán, whose fishermen sail to Arguineguín the following week.

P.133 ▸ The southwest coast

For an insight into the island's history and culture a trip to one of its many museums is highly recommended. Or if you're more interested in the visual arts, there are a couple of clean, modern exhibition spaces worth dragging yourself away from the beach for, which display changing exhibitions of the latest works from Europe, Africa and the Americas.

▲ Mundo Aborigen

The lost world of the pre-Hispanic Canarios is brought to life at this open-air folk museum on a stunning hilltop site.

P.120 ▸ The Costa Canaria

▼ Centro de Interpretación, Barranco de Guayadeque

This impressive museum, housed in a cave, explains the unique natural and cultural history of the island.

P.90 ▸ The east coast

▷ Casa de Colón

Learn about Columbus'
voyages of exploration and
the Canarian connection to
the New World.

P.53 ▸ Las Palmas:
Vegueta and Triana

◁ Museo Canario

Delve into the world of
the original Canarios,
with reconstructions
of their dwellings,
examples of pottery and
a creepy selection of
skulls and mummies.

P.55 ▸ Las
Palmas: Vegueta
and Triana

▷ Centro Atlántico de Arte Moderno

Expand your cultural
horizons at this cool,
cerebral and always
challenging gallery of
contemporary art.

P.52 ▸ Las
Palmas: Vegueta and
Triana

◁ Museo Néstor

The vibrant, sensuous
paintings of Néstor Martín-
Fernández de la Torre are the
focus of this enchanting small
museum.

P.68 ▸ Las Palmas:
Ciudad Jardín to La
Isleta

Churches

Most Canarian churches are simple affairs behind dignified Neoclassical or neo-Canarian facades. The exceptions are either much grander, as in the case of the imposing Catedral de Santa Ana in Las Palmas, or more modest, such as the exquisite Ermita de las Nieves in the island's northwest or the cave chapels at Guayadeque and Artenara. Very often, too, the church serves as the focus and chief landmark for a quiet and beautiful *casco historico*.

▼ Nuestra Señora del Pino

The most important pilgrimage church in the Canary Islands is stately without and suitably ornate within.

P.161 ▶ The north

▼ Ecumenical church of Playa del Inglés

A simple, elegantly modern symbol of spiritualism in the south of the island.

P.115 ▶ The Costa Canaria

▶ Ermita de las Nieves, Puerto de las Nieves

A little jewel at the heart of the island's loveliest fishing village.

P.150 ▶ The west coast and the Andén Verde

▶ Catedral de Santa Ana, Las Palmas

A beautiful but austere late Gothic building in dignified Neoclassical clothing.

P.54 ▶ Las Palmas: Vegueta and Triana

▼ San Juan Bautista, Arucas

Arucas' exuberant church blends Catalan flair with piety to impressive effect.

P.159 ▶ The north

▼ Cave churches

The cave chapels at Cueva Bermeja in the Barranco de Guayadeque and at Artenara exert a unique fascination.

P.80 ▶ The east coast and P.108 ▶ The Cumbre

Landmarks

Gran Canaria's landmarks are a mix of the natural and the man-made. Its most memorable features rise out of the island's dramatic volcanic landscape: the basalt sentinels dominating the island's centre, for instance, or the ice cream colours decorating the hillsides near Veneguera. But colour of a man-made variety turns a built-up hillside in Las Palmas into a startling landmark of a different kind, while the lighthouse at Maspalomas helps sun worshippers navigate the dunes.

▲ Faro de Maspalomas

This late nineteenth-century lighthouse predates all the south's modern tourist development.

P.117 ▶ The Costa Canaria

▲ Los Azulejos, Mogán

Ice cream colours splash across the hillsides in these vibrant, exposed rock strata in the island's southwest.

P.139 ▶ The southwest coast

▼ Roque Nublo

This giant basalt monolith is the symbol of the island's ruggedly beautiful heart.

P.104 ▶ The Cumbre

▼ Torre Woermann, Las Palmas

The shape of things to come in Las Palmas' regenerating port district.

P.73 ▶ Las Palmas: Ciudad Jardín to La Isleta

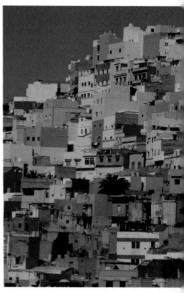

▲ Painted hillsides of Las Palmas

A vivid demonstration of the power of paint as colour sprawls across the hillside houses of a Las Palmas *barrio*.

P.56 ▶ Las Palmas: Vegueta and Triana

▲ Roque Bentayga

Geomorphology, history and spectacular scenery come together on this dramatic basalt peak in the heart of the Cumbre.

P.104 ▶ The Cumbre

Outdoor activities

Year-round good weather make the lure of the outdoors irresistible, and not just for sunbathing. Walking, climbing and jeep or camel rides offer a wonderful excuse to get out and discover the unspoilt parts of the island, while golf – already a major draw in Gran Canaria – is becoming ever more important as the island slowly takes its image up-market.

▲ Golf

Tee off on Gran Canaria's superb selection of courses both ancient and modern.

P.175 ▸ Essentials

▼ Hiking in the Pinar de Tamadaba

The peak of perfection for keen hikers in Gran Canaria's most outstanding pine forest.

P.108 ▸ The Cumbre

▼ A jeep safari in the mountains

Travel to steep and scary places you wouldn't dare drive yourself.

P.174 ▸ Essentials

▲ Explore the Jardín Canario

An entire island in one valley, from laurasilva and pine forest to dragon trees, coastal scrub and luxuriant non-native plants.

P.164 ▸ The north

▲ Camel rides

A bumpy reminder of the closeness of Africa, and of the island's past when camels were used as pack animals.

P.97 ▸ The Costa Canaria

Kids' Gran Canaria

Gran Canaria's big resorts have evolved on child-friendly lines, with many hotels having special children's entertainment or play facilities and with lots of parks and attractions guaranteed to keep kids of all ages amused. Las Palmas' Museo Elder is hi-tech, highly interactive and aimed specifically at children, while away from the coast, some of the more dramatic pre-Hispanic sites are sure to spark the young ones' imaginations.

▲ Sioux City

Rootin', tootin' cowboys, evil bandits and dancing saloon girls – but for many the stunt riders are the highlight.

P.114 ▶ The Costa Canaria

▲ Holiday World funfair

A good old-fashioned funfair with a big wheel and all the trimmings.

P.117 ▶ The Costa Canaria

◀ Water parks

Slides, spirals and pools mean there's plenty of fun to be had splashing and cooling off in the sun.

P.117, 118
▶ The Costa Canaria

▶ Gran Karting Club

With a separate track for 12–16 year olds and a miniature track for the tots, the island's go-karting circuit offers thrills without spills for all ages.

P.111 ▶ The Costa Canaria

▼ Palmitos Park

Performing parrots, flamingos, crocodiles and butterflies are among the attractions at this zoo and botanical garden.

P.118 ▶ The Costa Canaria

▲ Museo Elder, Las Palmas

Hands-on, engrossing and educational museum, with loads of interactive exhibits for kids to try out.

P.71 ▶ Las Palmas: Ciudad Jardín to La Isleta

Lesbian and gay Gran Canaria

For years Gran Canaria has been Europe's beach resort of choice for lesbians and gay men. With its vast infrastructure of bars, clubs, and apartments plus a splendid gay section of beach and dunes and the annual Gay Pride celebrations, it's no wonder many visitors never leave Playa del Inglés and Maspalomas, but Las Palmas in the north also has its scene – particularly exuberant at carnival time.

▲ The beach and dunes of Maspalomas

Legendary throughout Europe for its cruising and nude sunbathing. Just head for the beachfront snack bar number 7 where the gay crowds gather.

P.116 ▸ The Costa Canaria

▲ The Yumbo Centre

The concrete shopping centre that's home to Europe's largest single concentration of gay bars.

P.124 ▸ The Costa Canaria

◀ Gay Pride, Maspalomas

Floats, fun and grown men dressed as leopardskin handbags make for a very gay May.

P.125 ▶ The Costa Canaria

▶ Strand Apotheke, the Oasis, Maspalomas

Great beer and company and a superb view of the surfers on Maspalomas beach. Just watch out for the German *schlager* tunes.

P.130 ▶ The Costa Canaria

◀ Heaven, Playa del Inglés

An injection of London sophistication into the island's gay club scene.

P.130 ▶ The Costa Canaria

▶ Miau, Las Palmas

Go native for a real dose of latin spirit in the island's vibrant capital.

P.79 ▶ Las Palmas: Ciudad Jardín to La Isleta

Views

Gran Canaria's dramatic basalt peaks, its deep *barrancos* and volcanic craters, wild and rugged coast and spectacular beaches provide plenty of scenic thrills and photo opportunities.

▲ The Barranco de Moya

This green gorge is a spectacular surprise behind the town's modern church.

P.158 ▸ The north

▼ Caldera de Bandama

Vertigo-inducing views into a volcanic crater amid the vineyards and posh suburbia of Santa Brigida.

P.163 ▸ The north

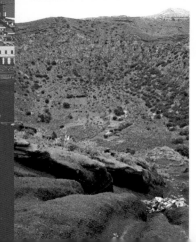

▶ Las Canteras Beach

One of Europe's best city beaches, right in the centre of Las Palmas.

P.71 ▶ Las Palmas: Ciudad Jardín to Las Isleta

◀ Dedo de Dios, Puerto de las Nieves

The "finger of god" was shorn of its topmost pinnacle by a tropical storm in 2005, but it's still the symbol of this fishing port.

P.149 ▶ The west coast and the Andén Verde

▶ Sunset over the dunes of Maspalomas from the Riu Palace hotel

Watching the sun setting over this mini-Sahara is the perfect end to a day at the beach.

P.116 ▶ The Costa Canaria

◀ The west coast from the Mirador del Balcón

The panoramas of the west coast from this lookout are truly breathtaking.

P.147 ▶ The west coast and the Andén Verde

Beaches

The golden dunes of Maspalomas and the elegant sandy curve of Playa de las Canteras are two of the great natural wonders of Gran Canaria – the former a mini-Sahara of shifting sands, the latter a superb city beach, animated from morning until night. The sunny resorts of the southwest have well-maintained, safe, artificial beaches, while elsewhere in the island the locals descend to the coast to enjoy the small sandy coves and their lively restaurants.

▲ Amadores

Beautiful, man-made Amadores is the broadest sweep of sand in Puerto Rico.

P.136 ▶ The southwest coast

▼ Montaña Arena

Proof that there are still secluded beaches even in the south, this quiet nudist beach is worth seeking out.

P.132 ▶ The southwest coast

▶ Sardina del Norte

This sheltered sandy cove is the locals' choice for sun, sand and seafood in the island's north-west.

P.152 ▶ The north

◀ Melenara, Telde

Great for people watching and for leisurely lunches by the sea, Telde's best beach is a clean sweep of dark sand.

P.83 ▶ Telde and around

▶ Playa de las Canteras, Las Palmas

This superb city beach and its calm, sheltered waters are perfect for sun, swimming and people watching.

P.71 ▶ Las Palmas: Ciudad Jardín to La Isleta

◀ Maspalomas

The endless golden sands of Maspalomas are the most amazing landscape feature in the south of the island.

P.118 ▶ The Costa Canaria

Watersports

Gran Canaria's breezy position creates excellent conditions for all kinds of watersports, and for windsurfing it's among the world's best destinations. Surfers can ride the Atlantic rollers, particularly in the north, while yachtsmen and women can follow in Columbus' wake. Scuba divers have pristine waters and sunken ships to explore, while for keen anglers the seas around the island teem with game fish.

▲ Windsurfing

Some of the best conditions for the sport in the world make Gran Canaria's east coast a major attraction for serious windsurfers and a popular place to learn the sport.

P.176 ▶ The east coast

▲ Canarian lateen sailing

Catch sight of the Canary Islands' tricky, indigenous form of sailing in the seas off Las Palmas, with regular regattas at weekends from April to October.

P.176 ▶ Essentials

▼ Scuba diving

Take a trip underwater to discover the hidden beauty of the seabed around the island.

P.175 ▸ Essentials

▼ Surfing and bodyboarding

There are dozens of spots to catch a wave, but the very best are in the north of the island.

P.157 ▸ Essentials

▲ Sailing

With fine weather, strong winds and plenty of marinas, Gran Canaria's waters are alive with sails.

P.176 ▸ Essentials

Places

Las Palmas: Vegueta and Triana

Stately, historic and a joy to explore, Vegueta and Triana are where Las Palmas began. It was at the mouth of the Barranco de Guiniguada in what is now Vegueta that on June 24, 1478 captain Juan Rejón set up a bridgehead for the Spanish conquest of the island. The fledgling city soon spread across the ravine to form Triana, from the start a commercial district in contrast to official and ecclesiastical Vegueta, though the city's growth was checked temporarily by a Dutch raid in 1599 that caused widespread destruction. Today, Vegueta is the island's most complete colonial city, dotted with lush, hidden patios and elaborate wooden balconies. It's also a place of government and home to the bulk of Las Palmas' cultural and architectural treasures – the cathedral, the Casa de Colón and the CAAM art gallery – as well as to many of its best bars. Triana has several fine examples of *Modernismo* architecture and is a major shopping district too, with small, often very chic boutiques. Like Vegueta it buzzes in the evening, especially around the Centro Comercial Monopol.

Avenida Marítima and Playa de la Laja

From Vegueta, the Avenida Marítima follows the coast south to the city's southern limits. Popular with joggers, it's dotted with public art and offers great views of ships queueing to enter the harbour. At its southern end is Las Palmas' quietest major city beach, the Playa de la Laja, a fine sandy affair stretching for 1.2km. Almost unknown to tourists, it attracts locals including fishermen who pull their boats up onto the sand, and surfers

---

Visiting Vegueta and Triana

Secure **parking** is available at the underground car park at Parque San Telmo opposite the city's main **bus station** (*estación de guaguas*). Vegueta and Triana are highly walkable but the yellow **guaguas municipales** – city buses are useful if you're visiting the Ciudad Jardín or continuing north to the port or beaches; #1 links Triana with the Ciudad Jardín and the port; #12 & 13 link Vegueta and Triana with the districts to the north, and #17 departs the Teatro Pérez Galdós northwards to Mesa y López and the Auditorio Alfredo Kraus. **Tourist information** is dispensed from distinctive kiosks at Parque San Telmo (Mon–Fri 10am–7.30pm, Sat 10am–3pm; ® www.promocionlaspalmas.com) and at Plaza Hurtado Mendoza close to the CC Monopol (same hours).

CAFÉS
Café & Bar Guiniguada **8**
Churrería-Chocolatería
Montesol **2**
El Perojo **1**
Pastelería Morales **3**

ACCOMMODATION
Hotel Madrid **C**
Hotel Parque **A**
Pensión Perojo **B**

N

BARS & CLUBS
CC Monopol **7**
Clicquot **15**
Floridita **6**
Jellyfish **9**
Scratch
Sports Bar **17**
Soul Train **14**
Tagoror **11**

SHOPS
El Gabinete
Gastronómico **a**
La Casa del Habano **b**

SAN NICOLÁS

RESTAURANTS
Casa Montesdeoca **13**
Cava de Triana **4**
Cho Zacarias **16**
El Herreño **10**
Hipócrates **12**

**LIVE MUSIC &
ENTERTAINMENT**
Cuasquías **5**

0   200 m

**LAS PALMAS:
VEGUETA & TRIANA**

ARENALES

Parque de
San Telmo

Estación
de Guaguas

Teatro
Cuayas

TRIANA

Casa Museo
Benito Pérez
Galdós

Teatro
Pérez
Galdós

Gabinete Literario

Mercado

Casa de Colón

CAAM

Catedral
Santa Ana

Casa Consortales

Museo Canario

Hospital de
San Martín

VEGUETA

Las Palmas: Vegueta and Triana   PLACES

and bodyboarders who come
for the waves. It isn't particularly
suitable for swimming, but a stroll
here on a fine windy day with
the Atlantic rollers pounding
the shore is an antidote to the
otherwise hectic pace of the
city. Global bus #55 for Jinamar,
many of the buses heading to the
southern resorts and city buses
#9, 12, 13 and 60 stop in the
district of Hoya de la Plata, linked
by footbridge to the beach.

CAAM (Centro Atlantico de Arte Moderno)

C/Los Balcones 11, Vegueta ⊛ www.
caam.net. Tues–Sat 10am–9pm,
Sun 10am–2pm. Free. Hidden
behind the imposing facade
of an eighteenth-century
mansion in one of Vegueta's
most elegant streets, the CAAM
is Las Palmas' major museum
of contemporary art. Instead
of a permanent collection, the
museum attracts international

touring exhibitions with the aim of highlighting the island's African, European and American cultural links. The exhibitions can be quite challenging, the white, modernist interior is cool and inviting and there's a well-stocked shop for stylish gifts and books. An annexe, the **Sala San Antonio Abad** (Plaza de San Antonio Abad; same hours, free) provides a more intimate space for smaller-scale exhibitions of modern art, including video work.

Casa de Colón

C/Colón 1, Vegueta @ www. grancanariacultura. com. Mon–Fri 9am–7pm, Sat & Sun 9am–3pm. Free. For a glimpse of colonial Las Palmas you should visit the Casa de Colón. This amalgam of three grand fifteenth-century houses is as old as anything in the city, its form reflecting Roman, Moorish and Andalucian influences and representing a prototype for the colonial architecture that spread from the Canary Islands to the Spanish colonies in the New World. Christopher Columbus stayed here in 1492 – in what was then the governor's house – in order to present his

credentials and to report that the rudder on one of his ships was broken. Unsurprisingly, the section of the museum that deals with Columbus is the most engrossing: a reconstructed section of one of his ships, *La Niña*, shows how frighteningly small they were. Upstairs there's a model of Las Palmas as it was in 1686, when Vegueta and Triana were separated by a stream and not, as now, by a busy road; plus a series of engravings of the Dutch attack on the city in 1599. The Gothic crypt contains exhibitions on

▲ CASA DE COLÓN

PLACES Las Palmas: Vegueta and Triana

pre-Colombian South American civilizations and there's a map of the Americas showing the settlements founded by Canary islanders. Close by, the tiny seventeenth-century chapel of **San Antonio Abad** stands on the spot where Juan Rejón set up his camp in 1478.

Catedral de Santa Ana

C/Obispo Codina 13, Vegueta.
Mon–Fri 10am–5pm, Sat 10am–2pm.
€3The Catedral de Santa Ana is Vegueta's greatest landmark. Begun around 1500 in the Gothic style, its construction was long and episodic, with various architects and eras leaving their mark on the structure, so that the Puerto del Aire (Door of Air) is Renaissance and the twin pulpits are Baroque. The building was finally completed with a Neoclassical facade in the nineteenth century. The Catedral is one of the most significant architectural monuments in the Canary Islands, thanks not just to its size and antiquity but above all to the beautiful late-Gothic interior, with its three naves of equal height. The forest of elegant columns and the looping vaulting are quite distinctive and reminiscent of a palm grove. Entry is via the **Museo Diocesano de Arte Sacro** (C/Espíritu Santo 20; same hours and ticket as Catedral), an extensive collection of religious art ranged around the beautiful, balconied seventeenth-century Patio de los Naranjos, a former orchard often heady with the scent of orange blossom. Among some fine woodcarvings and modernist stations of the cross, a gory eighteenth-century depiction of the martyrs of Tazacorte – 39 Portuguese Jesuits bound for Brazil who were killed by French corsairs off La Palma in 1570 – and a 1909 work by Néstor Martín-Fernández de la Torre, *Jesus entre los doctores de la iglesia*, stand out.

Plaza de Santa Ana

Laid out at the beginning of the sixteenth century, Plaza Santa Ana is a handsome square and the traditional heart of official Las Palmas, a fact reflected in its imposing if slightly austere architecture. Fringing the paved central space are some of the city's main architectural monuments: the Casa Regental (Regent's House), which dates back to the sixteenth century and is one of the few surviving Renaissance buildings in the city; the seventeenth-century Palacio Episcopal (Bishop's Palace) was rebuilt after the Dutch attack with a simple but harmonious facade; and the Neoclassical Casas Consistorales (City Hall), which dates from 1842. All these buildings remain in official use; the Casa Regental houses the Presidency of the Canary Islands Supreme Court. Bronze statues of dogs adorn the square, and there are benches to sit on and take in the historic surroundings. Open-air concerts and events sometimes take place here too.

Mercado de Vegueta

C/Mendizabal 1, Vegueta. Mon–Thurs 6.30am–2pm, Fri & Sat 6.30am–3pm. The oldest and most beautiful market in the city dates from 1854, and the wonderful displays of fresh fish, fruit and vegetables are well worth a browse. The presence of the market ensures that the surrounding streets are a hive of activity from early morning onwards, in contrast to the sleepy face much of Vegueta

▲ MERCADO DE VEGUETA

presents to the world. In the evenings, C/Mendizabal and C/La Pelota are transformed into the hub of Vegueta's convivial nightlife scene.

Museo Canario

C/Dr Verneau 2, Vegueta ⊛ www.elmuseocanario.com. Mon–Fri 10am–8pm, Sat & Sun 10am–2pm. €3. Founded in 1879, the Museo Canario explains the life and culture of the indigenous inhabitants of the island, the Canarios – a people of North African Berber origin – from 500 BC to the fifteenth-century conquest by the Spanish. It's an engrossing museum despite its somewhat stuffy and old-fashioned style; most exhibits are labelled in Spanish only, but an English language leaflet is available at the museum entrance. Exhibits include reconstructions of the burial mound of La Guancha, the El Pósito granary at Temisas and the famous Cueva Pintada (painted cave) at Gáldar, plus scale models of stone round houses and cave dwellings. Artefacts include the Ídolo de Tara, a red fertility sculpture that has become the symbol of Telde; Canario burial

ritual is demonstrated by the mummified corpse of a young man from Arguineguín and there are more than a thousand skulls. The section on pottery demonstrates the enduring influence of Canario styles on post-conquest earthenware.

Calle Dr Chil

The narrow stone canyon of C/Dr Chil is one Vegueta's most interesting streets, containing the old Augustinian convent that is now the High Court, the Baroque church of **San Francisco de Borja** and the austere **Seminario Conciliar**. The Jesuits established the Colegio de la Sagrada Familia in a house on this street in 1697 and in 1724 they began to build the church of San Francisco de Borja, the exterior of which is dominated by the flamboyant barley sugar columns flanking the door, while inside there's an eighteenth-century Rococo retable by José de San Guillermo. The Seminario Conciliar next door, established in 1777 in the former Jesuit Colegio, was the unlikely birthplace of the enlightenment in Gran Canaria's intellectual life.

Plaza del Espíritu Santo and around

C/Dr Chil continues west beyond the Museo Canario to the enchantingly pretty **Plaza del Espíritu Santo**, perhaps the loveliest of Vegueta's plazas, ranged around a tiny garden with a fountain beneath a stone baldachin at its centre. The plaza is fringed with stately colonial mansions and there's a chapel, the Ermita del Espíritu Santo. Continuing a little way along C/Castillo and C/Ramón y Cajal you soon reach a break in the buildings from which you can see the most impressive of Las Palmas' **painted hillsides**, actually the houses of the otherwise uninteresting Barrio San Nicolas which overlook the Barranco de Guiniguada from the north. Individually the houses are mostly not at all picturesque, but the coordinated colour scheme creates a memorable effect, particularly when bright sunshine emphasizes the vibrant shades used. On the south side of C/Ramón y Cajal stands the Hospital de San Martín, an imposing structure built to the plans of Colonel Antonio Lorenzo de la Rocha in 1775.

Church of Santo Domingo

Plaza de Santo Domingo, Vegueta. Dominating a broad, pleasantly shady square, the whitewashed Baroque church of Santo Domingo dates from the seventeenth century, when it was built to replace the original destroyed in the Dutch raid of 1599. Inside are some fine altarpieces and sculptures by the Canarian master Luján Pérez, though like many churches in Las Palmas it's usually locked except during mass. The stone fountain in the plaza outside also dates from the seventeenth century.

Teatro Pérez Galdós

Plaza de Stagno 1, Triana ☎928 361 509. Closed for modernization. This imposing theatre is named after the greatest Canarian writer, Benito Pérez Galdós, the "Spanish Dickens", who was born in Triana in 1843 (see p.58). The building is the work of Canarian architect Miguel Martín-Fernández de la Torre, who rebuilt it in 1918 after fire ravaged the original theatre dating from 1852. The interior includes frescoes by his brother, the symbolist painter Néstor Martín-Fernández de la Torre.

Alameda de Colón and the Plaza Cairasco

The raised, rectangular Alameda (boulevard) de Colón at the

▼ PLAZA DEL ESPIRITU SANTO

▲ TEATRO PÉREZ GALDÓS FRESCO

Iniciativas Culturales Caja de Canarias; ☎928 368 687), a multipurpose arts centre that incorporates a 400-seat theatre, occupies the nineteenth-century premises of the former *Hotel Negresco* on the opposite side of the square. The Alameda de Colón's northeast corner opens onto leafy, pedestrianized Plaza Cairasco, a popular spot for a drink at one of the pavement cafés beneath the palm trees. On the square are two of Triana's most historic buildings. The most prominent of these is the **Gabinete Literario** (☎928 364 658), an ornate fusion of nineteenth-century Neoclassicism and flamboyant *Modernismo* decoration. Founded as a literary society, its first president was a member of the British community, Roberto Houghton-Houghton. Today the building is used for a variety of events including dances; it's usually possible to get in to see the lofty entrance hall or to attend an event. To the right of the Gabinete Literario is the **Hotel Madrid**, with a dark, atmospheric and old-fashioned interior and a wide outdoor terrace that's good for

southern entrance to Triana is an attractive if busy open space that serves as a departure point for many of the municipal bus services. Watching over the comings and goings is the church of **San Francisco de Asis**, rebuilt in Baroque style in the seventeenth century after the 1518 original was destroyed in the Dutch raid of 1599. **CICCA** (Centro de

Franco in Gran Canaria

Francisco Franco Bahamonde was appointed military commandant of the Canary Islands by the Republican government early in 1936. Already known for his Right-wing sympathies, he wasn't trusted and it was felt wise to keep him far from Madrid, but the remoteness of Franco's posting did nothing to stop his plotting. On July 16, 1936 the military commander of Gran Canaria, Amado Balmes, was shot dead in mysterious circumstances whilst visiting a shooting range. His death gave Franco the pretext to travel overnight from his headquarters on Tenerife to Gran Canaria, where a chartered British plane was waiting to fly him to Spanish Morocco where the rebellion would begin. The Moroccan garrisons rose in revolt on the evening of July 17; Franco spent the night at the *Hotel Madrid* in Triana. Next morning he declared martial law, ordering the seizure of the post office, telephone and telegraph services, radio stations and utilities. The future dictator's manifesto was broadcast by a Las Palmas radio station. At 11am he set off for Gando airport by sea – the villages between the city and airport were controlled by his enemies – and at 2.15pm on July 18 Franco's plane took off for Morocco.

a civilized drink. It was in this hotel in 1936 that Franco spent his last night on Gran Canaria before joining the rebellion that became the Spanish Civil War.

Calle Mayor de Triana

Triana's long, traffic-free main street is considered a historical monument in its own right, such is the elegant impression created by the stately Neoclassical and beautiful *Modernismo* facades above its shops. It leads arrow straight from the Parque San Telmo in the north almost as far as the Guiniguada in the south, and is characterized by small and medium size boutiques, with a sprinkling of bars and cafés that keep the street scene lively well into the night.

Calle Cano

Narrower and more intimate than C/Mayor de Triana, C/ Cano is also distinctly more upmarket, one of a dense network of pleasant little streets which mix lovely *Modernismo* architecture with chic shopping and dining. Famous names in C/Cano itself include Mont Blanc and Cartier, while at no. 6 the **Casa-Museo Benito Pérez Galdós** (closed for restoration at the time of writing; scheduled to re-open during 2006; ☎928 366 976, ⓦwww.casamuseoperezgaldos) is the birthplace and childhood home of the man considered Spain's greatest writer after Cervantes and often compared to Dickens for his liberal views and sympathetic portrayal of the lower classes. The house itself is a very evocative slice of nineteenth-century Spanish bourgeois life, and includes furniture from the family homes in Madrid and Santander.

Parque San Telmo

Triana's northern edge is marked by the large, palm-shaded Parque San Telmo, a place of arrival and departure since the days when the city's original harbour was here. Today it's the bus station that is responsible for the never-ending parade of humanity. Solace comes in the shape of a wonderfully inventive children's play park, and there's a beautiful *Modernismo* café kiosk in the northwest corner. The plaza is also occasionally the venue for book

▲ CALLE CANO *MODERNISMO*

▲ HOUSES ON CALLE PEROJO

fairs and other special events. The oldest monument here is the low, whitewashed **Ermita de San Telmo**, which like several of the city's churches was destroyed during the Dutch raid of 1599 and rebuilt in the following century. If it happens to be open, inside there's a lovely Baroque retable. Parque San Telmo is overlooked on its west side by the stern Neoclassical facade (and armed military guards) of the Gobierno Militar, which dates from 1881. The north side of the plaza is occupied by the Bauhaus-style *Hotel Parque*, built in the early 1930s and still going; the east is separated from the ocean by the Avenida Marítima.

Cabildo Insular

C/Bravo Murillo 23, Triana. In stark contrast to the official buildings in Vegueta, the Cabildo Insular (Island Council) is a tour-de-force of clean, uncluttered interwar European Modernism, dating from 1932 and one of the most important examples of this architectural style in Spain. The architect was Miguel Martín-Fernández de la Torre, perhaps better known

for the neo-Canarian style of the Pueblo Canario in the Ciudad Jardín (see p.68) and the Teatro Pérez Galdós. Here, the influence of Le Corbusier and of the Bauhaus is clear.

Castillo de Mata

Carretera de Mata, between Avda Primero de Mayo and C/Bravo Murillo. This early seventeenth-century fortress is a surviving fragment of the fortifications that once defended the city from pirate attack. At the start of the twentieth century it was used as a barracks; today it is closed for renovation, pending future use as a cultural centre.

Barrio de Arenales

C/Bravo Murillo marks the northern limit of Triana, and for the most part the districts between here and the Ciudad Jardín are dull and worth skipping. However, a number of streets leading north from C/Bravo Murillo into the *barrio* of Arenales are enlivened by attractive, brightly coloured nineteenth-century town houses. Some of the best are to be seen on C/Perojo, and there's a groovy café-bar, *El Perojo*,

▲ EL GABINETE GASTRONÓMICO

on the corner of C/Murga at the far end of the street. Two important public buildings, the Gobierno Civil and the Comandancia de Marina, are on the Plaza de la Feria just to the north of here, where there's also a rather heroic-looking monument to Pérez Galdós. Fronting the Avenida Marítima behind the Comandancia de Marina is an eye-catching fountain, which is illuminated to spectacular effect at night.

Shops

El Gabinete Gastronómico

C/Torres 18, Triana ☎ 928 380 443. Mon–Fri 10am–2pm & 4.30–8.30pm, Sat 10am–2pm. Wonderful little wine merchant selling Spanish and Canarian wines including products from the Bodegas Monje in Tenerife, plus Canarian rums and imported whiskies and tobacco.

Fedac

C/Domingo J. Navarro 7, Triana ☎ 928 369 661, ✉ www.fedac.org. Mon–Fri 9.30am–1.30pm & 4.30–8pm. The Triana Fedac store is one of two government-backed outlets in the island (the other is in the south) selling traditional and modern handicrafts of excellent quality. An annexe, the Sala, displays a more limited selection of expensive designer items.

La Casa del Habano

C/Torres 22, Triana ☎ 928 433 496. Mon–Fri 9.30am–1.30pm & 4.30–8.30pm, Sat 10am–2pm. This award winning, atmospheric temple to tobacco is a cigar-lover's dream, with a humidor and a snug private smoking room. It only stocks leading Cuban brands including Cohiba and Montecristo.

Hotels & Pensions

Hotel Madrid

Plaza Cairasco 4, Triana ☎ 928 360 664. Dark wood, heavy plaster ceilings and a glazed internal patio add to the atmosphere of the *Hotel Madrid*, not the most luxurious hotel in the city but certainly the most historic (Franco stayed in room 3 here on the eve of the Spanish Civil War). Rooms at the front are nicest, spacious and with balconies and bathrooms, while those at the back are a little gloomy. €30–40.

Hotel Parque

C/Muelle de Las Palmas 2, Triana ☎ 928 368 000, ✉ www.hparque. com. This smart, air-conditioned and refurbished three-star hotel offers high standards of comfort and space for the money and the location couldn't be more convenient for exploring the island: it's right on the Parque San Telmo, opposite the Estacion de Guaguas and with the sights of Vegueta and Triana immediately accessible on foot. The views over the park are lovely; double glazing keeps the noise down. €67–79.

Pensión Perojo

C/Perojo 1, Arenales ☏928 371 387. Located in a lovely nineteenth-century building, *Pensión Perojo* has seventeen clean, airy rooms with shared bathrooms. It's basic but cheerful; the rooms have high ceilings, shutters and balconies, but given the central location not far from Parque San Telmo, you should reckon with some traffic noise. €24

Cafés

Café & Bar Guiniguada

1 Plaza Hurtada Mendoza, Triana ☏928 369 758. Mon–Fri 8.30am–midnight, Sat 11am–midnight. Strategically located between Vegueta and Triana and with outdoor tables facing the fountain and Moorish style kiosks of the plaza, this little café serves generous portions of somewhat Germanic cakes including apple strudel and poppy seed cheesecake, plus snacks and light meals, all at very reasonable prices.

Churrería-Chocolatería Montesol

C/Perojo 3, Arenales. Daily 6.30am–11pm. Most *churrerías* are rather grim, functional places, but not this one where the ceilings are high, there's a long zinc counter and the atmosphere is redolent of the 1950s. Early

mornings it's the place to enjoy traditional hot chocolate with *churros*, otherwise it's a cheap place to have a slice of tortilla, a plate of goat's cheese or a *café con leche*.

El Perojo

Mon–Fri 8.30am–12.30pm & Mon–Thurs 7.30pm–2am, Fri & Sat 7.30pm–3.30am. Cool, laid-back café-bar just north of Triana offering tapas and *bocadillos* throughout the morning and from early evening until late. It attracts a young and partly studenty crowd and gets livelier as the night wears on. There's also a giant TV screen showing football.

Pastelería Morales

C/Viera y Clavijo 4, Triana ☏928 380 782. Daily 9am–9pm. The most atmospheric of this small chain is all brown wood and genteel refinement and has a window at the back through which you can see bakers in silhouette The exquisite cakes, miniature *bocadillos* (filled rolls) and dainty sandwiches make this an excellent breakfast stop. The orange juice is good, too.

▲ CHOCOLATERÍA MONTESOL

Restaurants

Casa Montesdeoca

C/Montesdeoca 10, Vegueta ☎928 333 466. Mon–Sat 12.30–4pm & 8pm–midnight.

The delicacies at this well-known restaurant include flambéed giant prawns in champagne, sirloin steak béarnaise and stuffed piquillo peppers, but it's the stunningly beautiful setting in the patio garden of a grand old colonial house that is the key to its appeal. The ice cream flavoured with *gofio* and the honey and almond *bienmesabe* is delicious. Mains are around €15.

Cava de Triana

C/Travieso 35, Triana ☎928 381 302. Mon–Sat 12.30pm–1.30am. This elegantly casual modern wine bar and restaurant is a superb spot to enjoy Spanish wines and delicious, simply prepared tapas – around €6 a dish – or salads. The wine list is strong on Riojas, and the food includes dishes such as lamb with caramelized onions in balsamic, meltingly tender mixed sweet roast peppers and modish desserts which make inventive use of local ingredients such as *gofio* and *bienmesabe*.

Cho Zacarias

C/Audiencia 7, Vegueta ☎928 331 374. Tues–Sat 1–5pm & 8.30pm–midnight. Smart and fashionable restaurant in a lovely old house in the heart of Vegueta's main tourist zone. It's no tourist trap though, with food geared to sophisticated palates, including dishes such as duck ham salad with vinaigrette, pumpkin oil and mustard seeds and sea bass in cava with tagliatelle for €13–18.

El Herreño

C/Mendizábal 5, Vegueta ☎928 331 154. Daily 9.30–1am. Bustling and rather old fashioned, this big, traditional restaurant with its high stone arches and curved bar is a wonderful place to enjoy reasonably priced Spanish and Canarian specialities in an authentic atmosphere. The wine list includes many Canary Island bottles. If you choose to eat tapas style, try a *media ración* of the Herreño cheese.

Hipócrates

C/Colón 4, Vegueta ☎928 311 171. Tues–Fri 1.30–4pm & 7–8.30pm. Piquillo peppers and veggie couscous enliven the more predictable pasta and quiche-based fare at this pretty little vegetarian restaurant, located

▲ CAVA DE TRIANA

on a tiny but sunny patio opposite the Casa de Colón. There's also a *menú del día* for €9.

Bars

CC Monopol

A former hotel converted into a shopping centre, the Centro Comercial Monopol has evolved into the hub of Triana's nightlife. Until around midnight the action centres on the bars on the ground floor with their outdoor terrazas – particularly *Heineken* (Mon–Thurs noon–1.30am, Fri & Sat noon–2.30am, Sun noon–midnight) which serves tapas as well as draught and bottled beer, and its neighbour *Taberna Las Ranas* (Mon–Thurs noon–midnight, weekends noon–2.30am). As the night progresses, the action moves down the escalator to the centre's lower level, where a variety of bars – *Treinta y Tantos* for a 30 to 40-ish crowd, *Stiloko* for hip-hop fans, *Passion* and *Sister* for disco fans and *Babagee* and *Radio Mz 91.5* for a fashionable crowd – compete for custom and to outdo each other in decibels till around 4am at weekends.

Clicquot

C/Mesa de León 3, Vegueta. Fri & Sat 11pm–4.30am. The long, narrow main bar at this packed, vibrant, latino-pop hangout is overlooked by a balcony which promises some relief from the heaving 25–45 crowd; otherwise, expect to stand shoulder to shoulder with good-looking locals gyrating to Enrique Iglesias, Ricky Martin and the rest. Great fun.

▲ TAGOROR

Scratch Sports Bar

C/Obispo Codina 4, Vegueta. Mon–Wed 4pm–midnight, Thurs–Sat noon–2am, Sun noon–midnight. Bright, stylish bar that wears its sporting credentials relatively lightly, so the big screen might be showing Formula 1 racing or football but the soundtrack will likely be a mix of oldies and mainstream house. There's a 1970s retro feel to the decor, including plastic bucket chairs. Drinks prices are reasonable, and the crowd is smart and mostly over 25.

Tagoror

C/Mendizábal 23, Vegueta. Daily 8.30pm–2am. There's really no gimmick here and the decor is limited to a few framed prints of old Las Palmas, but *Tagoror* is regularly crammed to the doors with a chatty, diverse, rather cerebral student and academic crowd. Drinks are reasonably priced, and it's highly convivial. They also serve tapas.

Clubs

Floridita

C/Remedios 10–12, Triana. Mon–Wed 8pm–2.30am, Thurs 8pm–3.30am, Fri & Sat till 6am. Not-to-be-missed conversion of a grand old house complete with a garden full of luxuriant palms out back. The atmosphere is latin and Caribbean, the drinks of choice mojitos or daiquiris and the music, at its best, pure salsa. It attracts a dressed up, mainstream, 30- to 40-something crowd who come here to dance. No cover, but drinks are expensive.

Jellyfish

C/La Pelota 16, Vegueta. Mon–Wed 9pm–3.30am, Thurs–Sat 9pm–4.30am. Very cool DJ bar, spread over several floors, that's spacious, modern and buzzy, with plenty of people dancing on the lower level but getting more lounge-like and laid-back as you ascend. The music is mainstream house, the crowd is 25–45 and the toilets unisex. Drinks prices are at club levels.

Soul Train

C/Mendizábal 37, Vegueta. Thurs–Sat 11.30pm–4am. This dark, sexy DJ bar is devoted to black music, majoring in R&B but encompassing funk and soul.

There's plenty of room for the young crowd to dance as well as a more intimate upper bar for getting to know each other better. Drinks are cheaper before 1.30am.

Live music & entertainment

Cuasquías

C/San Pedro 2, Triana ☎928 370 046. Tues–Sat 11pm–3am; live music generally starts around 12.30am. Triana's main venue for live bands is a vast place built around a glazed courtyard, with scrubbed stone walls, a couple of pool tables and an atmospheric, high-ceilinged bar. It ticks over during the week but is crowded at weekends, and the music varies from jazz and singer-songwriters to rock and funk.

Teatro Cuyas

C/Viera y Clavijo, Triana ☎928 432 180, ☻www.teatrocuyas.com. Tucked behind the facade of a former cinema in Triana, the Teatro Cuyas is currently the city's leading venue for theatre and musicals as well as a venue for classical music, ballet and contemporary dance, including the annual festivals of *zarzuela* – Spanish operetta – and opera.

Las Palmas: Ciudad Jardín to La Isleta

Intensely urban and effortlessly cosmopolitan, northern Las Palmas is a creation of the late nineteenth and twentieth centuries, when the rapid rise of shipping and tourism turned the capital of Gran Canaria into the largest city in the Canary Islands. Sprawling across a low-lying isthmus, it's a fascinating mix of the raucous and the refined: on its western flank there's a truly exceptional city beach, the Playa de las Canteras, backed by luxury hotels and an elegant modern concert hall; to the east, the vast artificial harbour of Puerto de la Luz sees a steady stream of cruise liners, warships, deep-sea trawlers and cargo ships of all kinds. The streets in between are lively around the clock with the action focusing on the Parque Santa Catalina, home to Las Palmas' annual Carnival and year-round nightlife, and the Avenida José Mesa y López, the city's principal shopping street. To the north, La Isleta offers great surfing and excellent views of the city from its volcanic hills, while to the south the classy residential Ciudad Jardín (Garden City) has a leafy elegance and a cultural scene centred on the Pueblo Canario in the sub-tropical Parque Doramas.

Distinguished by its tree-lined avenues and opulent late nineteenth-century villas, the Ciudad Jardín has long been a well-to-do neighbourhood, strongly associated with the city's British community, which a century ago played a major part in Gran Canaria's economic development – the district was once known as the *Barrio de los Ingleses*.

▼ PARQUE DORAMAS

Parque Doramas and around

Parque Doramas is a compact but lush public park grouped around fountains and planted with native Canary Island species as well as some of the

LAS PALMAS: CIUDAD JARDÍN TO LA ISLETA

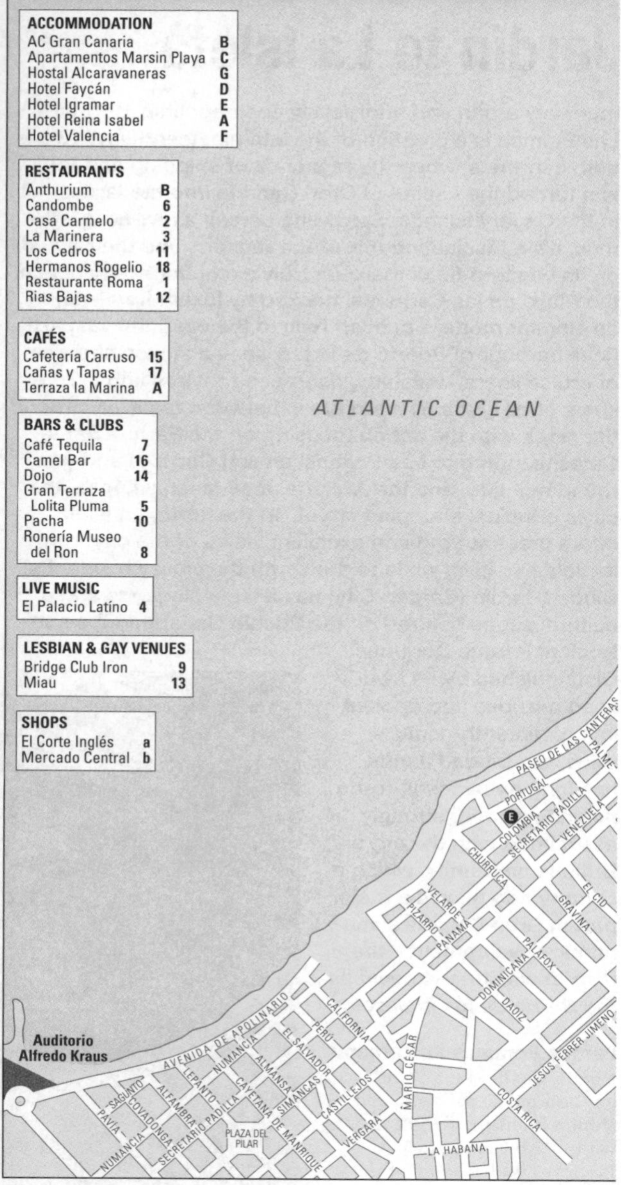

ACCOMMODATION

AC Gran Canaria	B
Apartamentos Marsin Playa	C
Hostal Alcaravaneras	G
Hotel Faycán	D
Hotel Igramar	E
Hotel Reina Isabel	A
Hotel Valencia	F

RESTAURANTS

Anthurium	B
Candombe	6
Casa Carmelo	2
La Marinera	3
Los Cedros	11
Hermanos Rogelio	18
Restaurante Roma	1
Rias Bajas	12

CAFÉS

Cafetería Carruso	15
Cañas y Tapas	17
Terraza la Marina	A

BARS & CLUBS

Café Tequila	7
Camel Bar	16
Dojo	14
Gran Terraza Lolita Pluma	5
Pacha	10
Ronería Museo del Ron	8

LIVE MUSIC

El Palacio Latíno	4

LESBIAN & GAY VENUES

Bridge Club Iron	9
Miau	13

SHOPS

El Corte Inglés	a
Mercado Central	b

ATLANTIC OCEAN

Auditorio
Alfredo Kraus

PASEO DE LAS CANTERAS
PALMERA
PORTUGAL
SECRETARIO PADILLA
VENEZUELA
COLOMBIA
CHURRUCA
EL CID
GRAVINA
VELARDE
LISZT
PANAMÁ
ALFARO
PALAZÓN
DOMINICANA
DAOIZ
JESÚS FERRER JIMÉNO
MARIO CÉSAR
COSTA RICA
AVENIDA DE APOLINARIO
JACINTO
NUMANCIA
ALFAMBRA
LEPANTO
COVADONGA
SECRETARIO PADILLA
PERÚ
CALIFORNIA
EL SALVADOR
ALMANSA
SIMANCAS
CAFETERÍA DE MANRIQUE
CASTILLEJOS
VERGARA
LA HABANA
PAVIA
NUMANCIA
PLAZA DEL PILAR

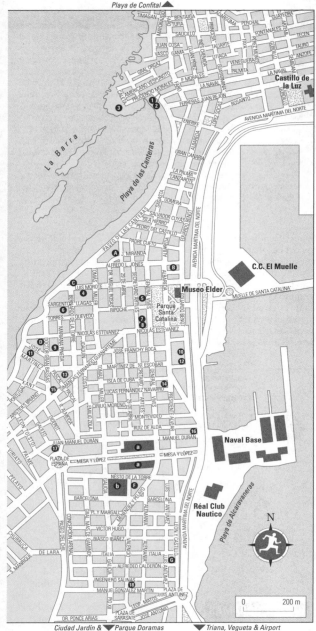

Playa de Confital

La Barra

Playa de las Canteras

Castillo de la Luz

C.C. El Muelle

Museo Elder

Muelle de Santa Catalina

Parque Santa Catalina

Naval Base

Réal Club Nautico

Playa de Alcaravaneras

N

0   200 m

Ciudad Jardín & ▼ Parque Doramas   ▼ Triana, Vegueta & Airport

Visiting northern Las Palmas

Las Palmas isn't a relaxing city for drivers, but secure **parking** is available (at a price) at the *Hotel Santa Catalina* and in the multistorey car parks close to Parque Santa Catalina, which is also the chief bus terminus for the north of the city. Most of this part of the city is walkable, but the yellow *guaguas municipales* are useful if you're visiting the Ciudad Jardín or continuing south to Vegueta or Triana. Bus #1 serves the Ciudad Jardín and Triana; #17 travels along the waterfront as far as the Teatro Pérez Galdós in Triana; buses #12 and #13 continue beyond Triana to Vegueta and buses #2 and #25 are useful if you're travelling between the shopping districts of Avda. Mesa y López and Triana. **Tourist information** is dispensed from booths on Avda. Mesa y López, at Parque Santa Catalina and opposite the *Hotel Meliá Las Palmas* on the Paseo Canteras (Mon–Fri 10am–7.30pm, Parque Santa Catalina and Paseo Canteras also Sat 10am–3pm; ֎ www.promocionlaspalmas.com).

The municipal bus company also operates a hop-on, hop-off sightseeing bus, the *guagua turistica*, which departs from Parque Santa Catalina (every 30 minutes; 9.30am–5.45pm); buy your ticket on board.

luxuriant non-native flowering specimens that flourish here, including jacaranda and roses. On the south side of the park stands the **Pueblo Canario**, designed by Miguel Martín-Fernández de la Torre in 1939, a complex of low buildings in neo-Canarian style, grouped around a plaza in which, on

Sundays, traditional folk dances are performed. There's a café and a shop selling handicrafts. The Pueblo's centrepiece is the **Museo Néstor** (Tues–Sat 10am–8pm; Sun & hols 10.30am–2.30pm; €2) opened in 1956 as a permanent home for the works of Miguel's brother, the painter Néstor Martín-Fernández de la Torre, who died in 1938. Néstor's work was uniquely Canarian, using strong colours and motifs – fruit, children and tropical birds – to summon up his Canary Island home from his studio in Madrid. The collection's high points are the eight paintings of the *Poem of the Sea*, and the unfinished *Poem of the Land*, while his etchings and drawings reveal a draughtsman of considerable confidence, and his tourist posters of 1930s Gran Canaria are fascinating. Alongside the Pueblo Canario stands the **Hotel Santa Catalina**, Gran Canaria's only example of a traditional palace hotel, which owes its current

▲ Las Canteras & La Isleta

0   100 m

N

ACCOMMODATION
Hotel Santa Catalina   A

RESTAURANTS
Bodegon del
Pueblo Canario   1

TONY CASTILLO
BRASIL
LEOPARDI
GAGO COUTINHO
AVENIDA MARÍTIMA DEL NORTE
ALEJANDRO HIDALGO
BEETHOVEN
PLAZA
EMILIO
LEY
LEÓN CASTILLO
Parque
Doramas
A
1
EMILIO LEY
MADRID
PASEO DE
ÁNGEL GUIMERÁ
JUAN CARLO
PASEO DEL CHIL
PASEO DE LUSO
AVENIDA DE JUAN XXIII
J. DEL RIVERO
PASEO DEL TOMÁS MORALES

Triana & Vegueta

PARQUE DORAMAS

▲ MUSEO NÉSTOR

Alcaravaneras

The *barrio* of Alcaravaneras is home to the city's central market and the island's football stadium, but despite this it's a surprisingly low-key neighbourhood, its tight grid of quiet residential streets slowly losing their remaining early twentieth-century houses as newer, bigger apartment blocks take their place. The main draw is the broad **Playa de las Alcaravaneras**, a 550-metre strip of pristine gold sand wedged between the Muelle Deportivo and the Real Club Náutico de Gran Canaria, one of Las Palmas' three yacht clubs. Given its position by the port, this isn't the most alluring place for a swim, but it's a popular spot for beach sports, including volleyball and football, and for wet biking and windsurfing.

grandiose appearance to remodelling work by Miguel Martín-Fernández de la Torre. Financed by the British-owned Grand Canary Islands Company and originally opened in 1890, it remains a pleasant place to take tea. For accommodation details see p.75. The hotel also houses the **Casino Las Palmas** (C/León y Castillo 227 ☎928 233 908, ⓦwww. casinolaspalmas.com; Sun–Thurs 4pm–4am; Fri & Sat 4pm–5am; passport or ID required for entry). Across the busy Avenida Marítima from the hotel is the **Muelle Deportivo**, Las Palmas' main yacht marina, currently being upgraded.

▲ PLAYA DE LAS ALCARAVANERAS

▲ PARQUE SANTA CATALINA

Avenida José Mesa y López

From the Real Club Náutico in the east to the Plaza España in the west, the arrow-straight main section of the Avenida José Mesa y López is Las Palmas' principal shopping street and the home to its biggest stores, including Mango, Zara, Cortefiel, Marks & Spencer and the gargantuan twin buildings of the El Corte Inglés department store. Though the avenue is permanently clogged with traffic

there's a pleasant tree-lined paseo down the middle, and the Plaza España is a popular spot to linger, with many *terrazas* that stay busy late into the evening.

Parque Santa Catalina

Parque Santa Catalina is the social and entertainment centre of Las Palmas. The large, rectagonal open space is more plaza than park, its tall palms overtopped by the *AC Hotel*, its western side lined with

Carnival in Las Palmas

Carnival (*carnaval* in Spanish) is the most important festival of the year in Las Palmas. Enthusiastically celebrated with live music and ridiculous costumes for several weeks in the late winter, there's something on almost every night and the morning papers lead on Carnival-related news. Though its origin is in the traditional Catholic pre-Lent carnival, nowadays the timetable is only loosely related to the religious calendar and festivities sometimes continue even after the traditional last day of Ash Wednesday. For the duration of Carnival the **Parque Santa Catalina** is taken over by a giant outdoor stage decorated with that year's theme, which can be anything from Don Quixote to the Far East or Latin America. Major events include the selection of the Carnival Queen and of the Drag Queen of Carnival, both of which are all-ticket events but are televised live. Most nights of the week during Carnival there's something going on in Parque Santa Catalina and, whether you dress up or not, it's easy to enjoy the carnival spirit. The Burial of the Sardine (Entierro de la Sardina) marks the end of Carnival: tens of thousands follow a giant effigy of a sardine through the city's streets from Parque San Telmo in Triana to the beach at Las Canteras, many wearing the costumes of the amateur marching bands that are a fixture of the carnival season or dressed as weeping widows. When the procession reaches the beach, an honour guard places the sardine on an offshore platform and it is burnt. A spectacular firework display then brings the festivities to an end for another year. For more information on proceedings check out ⊛ www.laspalmascarnaval.com.

pavement cafés and the more open eastern side by former warehouses now converted to cultural and leisure use. One of these, the **Museo Elder** (entrance on Plaza Comandante Ramón Franco; Tues–Sun 10am–8pm; ❂www.museoelder. org; €5) is the most child-friendly attraction in Las Palmas, a highly interactive science and technology museum with everything from a cutaway Smart Car to environmentally-themed displays and a hands-on exploratorium – some of the exhibits are labelled in English – plus an IMAX cinema on the top floor with one showing daily in English with prior notice. Throughout the year festivals and live performances from Carnival to WOMAD use the *parque* as their main stage, and it's a rare week when there isn't something of interest going on. By day, the streets between the square and the Playa de las Canteras are animated by the comings and goings from the beach and by the dozens of Indian-owned electrical shops – a feature here since the 1960s. By night, the area holds the biggest concentration of

nightlife in Las Palmas, with everything from restaurants and salsa clubs to chillout lounges, gay bars and a sizeable red-light element. Note that as the night wears on parts of the area develop a sleazy edge.

Playa de las Canteras

West-facing, 3km-long Playa de las Canteras is one of Europe's truly great city beaches, protected by an offshore reef, La Barra, that makes it safe for swimming, and backed by the traffic-free Paseo Canteras, which offers plenty of opportunities for people-watching and café lounging. On hot weekend afternoons, the beach becomes Las Palmas' front room; in the evening, the sunset stroll along the promenade is popular with visitors and locals alike. For most of its length the beach is of fine, golden sand, with just the very southern end, where the sea conditions are rougher and surfers and bodyboarders congregate, consisting of the black sand more characteristic of Tenerife. The excellent facilities include showers, changing rooms, umbrella hire

▲ PLAYA DE LAS CANTERAS

and hammocks. Las Canteras was once the most important tourist beach on the island, but package tourism slowly shifted to the more reliably sunny south in the 1960s and 1970s, and it has since assumed a more local character.

La Isleta

The northern limit of Las Palmas is marked by the distinctive, rounded volcanic hills of La Isleta, a thinly settled and largely barren landscape almost devoid of vegetation but with good surfing possibilities on the coast and, from its heights, wonderful views back to the city. The nicest approach to the area is along the attractive clifftop promenade that starts from the rocky headland of La Puntilla at the north end of the Playa de las Canteras and winds its way past rocky coves popular with local bathers. At the far end, a rough track leads down to the rocky **Playa del Confital**, packed out with surfers at weekends thanks to the best right-hand wave on the island. Beyond

it stretches the distinctive volcanic moonscape of La Isleta itself. Much of it is given over to a military base, but there is a residential district, Las Coloradas, from which a stoney and indistinct path leads past five-a-side football pitches to a superb view of Las Canteras' full sweep. Bus #41 goes to Las Coloradas from Santa Catalina.

Puerto de la Luz

Las Palmas' port was built in the second half of the nineteenth century to the plans of Juan de León y Castillo, the engineer responsible for the lighthouse at Maspalomas and whose life is commemorated by a museum in his home town of Telde (see p.80). It's the largest port in the Canaries and one of Spain's biggest, a major transit point between Europe, Africa and the Americas. Besides ferry and hydrofoil links to mainland Spain and the other Canary Islands, it is a significant cruise liner port. The best views are from the outdoor *terraza* bars on the upper floors of the **El Muelle** shopping centre, which

▲ EL MUELLE

overlooks the cruise liner pier. Despite opposition from some residents, the city port authority and Cabildo Insular (Island Council) are pressing ahead with plans for extensive redevelopment to link the port more closely to the tourist district behind Las Canteras. The architect Cesar Pelli, who designed the Petronas Towers in Kuala Lumpur, was joint winner of a design competition early in 2005. For now, the El Muelle centre and the ultra-modern, tilting Torre Woermann skyscraper are the main symbols of regeneration.

Overlooking the port from the north the **Castillo de la Luz** is a squat fortress that was built at the time of the Spanish conquest and extended in the seventeenth century. Surrounded by a small but attractive park, in the past it served as a cultural centre, but is currently undergoing restoration and not open to the public.

Shops

El Corte Inglés

Avenida José Mesa y López 15 & 18 ☎928 263 000, ✆www.elcorteingles. es. Mon–Sat 10am–10pm. Gran Canaria's largest department store is housed in two mammoth modern buildings that face each other across the Avenida José Mesa y López. The building on the north side of the avenue contains the fashion departments, a gourmet store on the second floor and a large basement food hall with spectacular displays of fish and ham, plus plenty of foodie treats that make good gifts. The other building contains housewares, books, stationery, music and a newsagent's stall.

Mercado Central

Calle Galicia. Open Mon–Sat 7am–2pm. Las Palmas' largest market lacks the picturesque architecture of the market in Vegueta, but it has the same mix of excellent fish, meat, vegetable and deli stalls making it the ideal place to assemble a cheap picnic, and at the back of the 1950s building there's also a *churrería* for the traditional clubber's breakfast of hot chocolate with *churros*.

Hotels

AC Gran Canaria

C/Eduardo Benot 3 ☎902 292 293, ✆www.ac-hotels.com. Towering 26 storeys above the Parque Santa Catalina, this distinctive, circular hotel is a spectacular example of 1970s architecture, its brutalist profile softened by geometric motifs cast into the concrete. It has a rooftop swimming pool and a restaurant spread over the 23rd and 24th floors offering stunning views over the city and Atlantic. Refurbishment has created a stylish contemporary city hotel, more business- than tourist-oriented but very convenient for the beach. The bedrooms sport elegant, dark colour schemes, wood floors and excellent bathrooms. Non-smoking rooms are available. Air conditioned. €85.

Hostal Alcaravaneras

C/Luis Antúnez 22 ☎928 248 914, ✆www.canaryhostel.com. Basic but clean and friendly, with some en-suites and TV in all rooms, this hostel is a good budget option. The location is central without being too noisy: it's tucked into a residential district close to Avenida Mesa y López and the Playa de Alcaravaneras, with bus stops, neighbourhood restaurants and the market close by. €22.

Hotel Faycán

C/Nicolás Estévanez 61 ☏938 270 650, ⊛www.hotelfaycan.com. Convenient for Las Canteras beach and Parque Santa Catalina, the *Faycán* is a spacious, clean, well-maintained three-star hotel, with comfortable if slightly old-fashioned rooms in 1960s style for up to three people, plus a few singles and rooms for four. Rooms have satellite TV, fridge and telephone; bathrooms are smart, and some studios have kitchens. €51.

Hotel Igramar

C/Colombia 12 ☏928 472 960, ⊛www.igramar.com. Officially rated three stars, this recently refurbished, air-conditioned hotel at the quieter, southern end of Las Canteras represents exceptionally good value for the standard of comfort and decor on offer. Doubles are furnished in tasteful boutique hotel style, many with floor to ceiling windows and Juliet balconies; there are also a few singles and triples decorated to the same high standard. Bathrooms are smartly finished in tile and granite. The Paseo Canteras and the beach itself are only a few metres away. €60.

Hotel Reina Isabel

C/Alfredo L. Jones 40 ☏928 260 100, ⊛www.bullhotels.com. This comfortable four-star hotel has a stunning location right on the seafront overlooking the Playa de Las Canteras. Many rooms have wonderful sea views, though cheaper ones have rather less wonderful vistas of the narrow street behind the hotel. The decor throughout is smart if not particularly trendy – it was last refurbished in 1996 – and all rooms are air-conditioned with TV, telephone, radio, en-suite bathroom and balcony. There's a rooftop swimming pool and a popular café facing the promenade. €96.

▲ HOTEL SANTA CATALINA

Hotel Santa Catalina

C/Léon y Castillo 227 ☎928 243 040, ⊛www.hotelsantacatalina.com. Standing in splendid isolation amid the palms of the Parque Doramas, this five-star, luxury hotel is of the old school and the traditional choice of visiting VIPS: past guests have included Prince Charles, Maria Callas and the Spanish royal family. The imposing architecture and grand decor of the public areas are matched in the rooms and suites, which are furnished in traditional style. Facilities include a spa and indoor and outdoor saltwater pools, and there's golf available for guests at the El Cortijo course just south of the city. €197.

Hotel Valencia

C/Valencia 4 ☎928 292 584, ℻928 230 929. In a very central position on a side street close to the Mercado Central and the shops of Avenida Mesa y López, the *Valencia* is a bright, attractive two-star hotel furnished in 1960s style, with spacious, comfortable doubles plus a few singles and triples, all with bath. Some rooms have balconies. Breakfast is not included, but there are plenty of affordable eating places nearby. €45.

Apartments

Apartamentos Marsin Playa

Luis Morote 54 ☎928 270 808, ⊛www.marsinplaya.com. These simple but clean and bright apartments are block-booked by Scandinavian travel agents during the winter months but are available at bargain prices from mid-April to the end of October. The complex is located right on the Playa de Las Canteras and many of the apartments have a sea view. Each sleeps 2–3 and has kitchen, telephone, bathroom and either terrace or balcony. €33.

Cafés

Bar Carabela

Hotel Santa Catalina, Avda Léon y Castillo 227. Daily 10am–1am. The bar and veranda of the *Hotel Santa Catalina* is a wonderfully atmospheric place to stop for a light meal or drink, thanks to the impressive architecture of the old hotel, the lush setting in the Parque Doramas and the urbane, efficient service. The chicken club sandwich is very generous, the tea good and prices surprisingly reasonable.

Cafetería Carruso

Plazoleta de Farray 5 ☎928 222 694. Daily 8.30am–1 or 2am. This cheap and cheerful neighbourhood café is one of a number on the pleasant little Plazoleta de Farray, where you can eat al fresco under the palms and listen to the plashing of the fountain or the laughter of children playing. Prices start at around €2 for a sandwich, while the *platos combinados* offer a hearty approximation to an Anglo-Saxon fry-up.

Cañas y Tapas

Plaza de España 5. Daily 8am–midnight. Part of a national chain, this Madrileño-style tapas bar is one of a number of bars and *terrazas* on the plaza, which is a popular spot to sit and watch the traffic go by. It serves reasonably-priced toasted sandwiches, salads and tapas plus more elaborate set menus. The beers include Kronenbourg and San Miguel.

Terraza la Marina

Hotel Reina Isabel, C/Alfredo L. Jones 40 ☎ 928 260 100. Daily 10.30am–midnight. The seafront terrace of the posh *Reina Isabel* hotel is the prime spot for swanky café lounging on the Paseo de las Canteras. They make a decent pot of tea, there's a full bar, plenty of shade and sooner or later everyone in Las Palmas walks past here. On Sundays they prepare paella here right in front of the diners. Prices are reasonable.

Restaurants

Anthuriun

AC Gran Canaria, C/Eduardo Benot 3 ☎ 928 244 908. Daily 1.30–3.20pm & 8.30–11.30pm. The sweeping views over the city and the Atlantic from this smart modern restaurant are highly memorable, while the food is a fusion of traditional Canarian and Catalan cuisine with more modern influences, so that you might dine on tuna with pistachio *mojo* or lamb chops with couscous and coriander pesto. Mains cost €15 and up. There's a more intimate sister restaurant at C/Pi y Margall 10 in Alcaravaneras.

Bodegón del Pueblo Canario

Pueblo Canario, Parque Doramas ☎ 928 242 985. Daily 11am–midnight; restaurant 11am–4pm & 7–11pm. With its broad terrace taking up much of the courtyard of the Pueblo Canario, this is one of the relatively sparse dining options in this largely residential part of town. The food – *calamares a la Romana*, *papas arrugadas*, fresh fish and the like – is good, if not especially cheap at €3.50–7 for tapas dishes. They have traditional Canarian folk dancing shows here on Sundays from 11.30am–1pm

Candombe

C/Sargento Llagas 43 ☎ 928 270 565. Daily 1–5pm & 8pm–midnight, Fri & Sat till 1am. There's no real choice at this popular, lively Brazilian *churrascaría* except how much to eat – the delicious grilled meat just keeps coming until you tell them to stop. This is the only restaurant in the island serving the cuisine of Rio Grande do Sul, Brazil's southernmost state: the meat is carved from long skewers at the table, and it's all rather theatrical. Don't fill up on the warm bread, delicious dips or excellent salads if you want to get full value from the €16 set price menu.

Casa Carmelo

Paseo de las Canteras 2 ☎ 928 469 056. Daily 1–5pm & 8pm–midnight. Exceptionally delicious *morcilla* (blood sausage) and simply but beautifully prepared steaks are the stock in trade of this

▲ PUEBLO CANARIO

well-known restaurant at the northern end of the Paseo de las Canteras, though they also do mountainous salads. Service is efficient, if a little abrupt at times, and you can expect to pay around €13 for a main course.

Hermanos Rogelio

C/Manuel González Martín 36, corner C/Valencia ☎928 248 680. Daily 12.30–5.30pm & 7.30pm–12.30am. This pleasant, unpretentious Alcaravaneras restaurant is a good place to dine tapas-style for around €9 a dish. The *papas arrugadas* are particularly fine, the *pulpo a la gallega* (octopus with paprika and olive oil) generous and two *media raciones* each should be enough for all but the most ravenous. The brothers' empire has colonized three out of four corners of the intersecting streets outside, so the formula clearly works.

La Marinera

La Puntilla, Paseo de las Canteras ☎928 468 802. Daily 1pm–2am. It may not be the best fish restaurant in Las Palmas, but this sister to *Casa Carmelo* certainly has the most beautiful site, among the rock pools at the northern end of the Playa de las Canteras. Come around sunset, stick to whatever's fresh and simple – the fancier concoctions don't always convince – and you should have a memorable meal. €3–6 for tapas, €11 for mains.

Los Cedros

C/Martínez de Escobar 68 ☎928 269 667. Tues–Sun 1–4.30pm & 7.30pm–12.30am. The Ibiza-style dance music soundtrack makes an interesting contrast to the 1960s tourist posters of Beirut and Baalbek at this pleasantly old-fashioned Lebanese restaurant, just a few steps from Canteras

beach. It's one of the best bets for veggies in the north of the city, since you can feast mezze style on the likes of *fatoush*, *babaganoush* or *tabbouleh* without the need to resort to meat. That said, the lamb is rather good. Mains cost €7.

Restaurante Roma

Paseo de las Canteras 1 ☎928 486 112. Open 1–4.30pm & 8pm–12.30am. Solid, traditional Italian restaurant right on the beachfront at the north end of the Paseo Canteras, with kitschy murals and a good selection of pizza and fresh pasta dishes, plus sea views from some tables.

Rias Bajas

C/Simón Bolivar 3, Edificio Saba ☎928 273 461. Daily 1–4pm & 8pm–midnight. The tank full of live crustacea takes pride of place in this long-established and well-regarded Galician fish restaurant close to the port. The atmosphere is a little snooty and traditional – so smart dress is a good idea – and you should expect to pay around €20 for a fish main course.

Bars

Café Tequila

C/Secretario Artiles 44. Tues–Sun 8pm–2.30am. This trendy newcomer bills itself as a chillout café, which might have something to do with the tequila – around €5 with mixer – but might equally be due to the subdued lighting, soft colour scheme and comfortable seating; there's even a giant bed out back. The soundtrack is R&B and there's space to dance up front.

The Camel Bar

C/León y Castillo 389. Mon–Sat 8pm–2.30am. One of the most popular bars in the area, the *Camel Bar* is decorated with camel heads and other references to the famous cigarette brand and attracts a young, boisterous, if mainstream crowd, who seem to go for the chart sounds on the playlist.

Gran Terraza Lolita Pluma

Parque Santa Catalina. Daily 9.30am–1.30am. A handy pit stop for a light snack or beer on Parque Santa Catalina, this *terraza* is also a slice of local colour. The name recalls a well-known local eccentric, Lolita Pluma (Lolita Feather in English), who eked out a living selling chewing gum to tourists whilst caring for the local street cats, and who was known for her exotic dress sense and lurid make-up. She died in 1988, but her portrait still adorns the outside wall.

Ronería Museo del Ron

C/Secretario Artiles 42 ☎ 928 265 200. Mon–Sat 9.30pm–late. This is the obvious place to order a *mojito* in Las Palmas, since getting pleasantly blurred on one of 300 rums from 25 countries is the whole purpose of this spacious bar. They stock every variety produced in Gran Canaria itself, the "Treasure Island" decor is

fun and there's no shortage of places to sit and chat for the diverse, convivial crowd. A Cuba Libre (rum and coke) will cost around €5.50; they also sell Cuban cigars.

Clubs

Dojo

C/Presidente Alvear 69 ☎ 928 492 585, ⊛ www.dojolaspalmas.com. Thurs–Sat 12.30–5am. One of the newest and hippest clubs in the north of Las Palmas, with cool decor, eye-catching podium dancers and a changing array of inventive themed events, including 60s, 70s and 80s nights and Ibiza-style white parties. Flyers and downloads from the club website give free drinks and two-for-one offers.

Pacha

C/Simón Bolivar 3 ☎ 928 271 684. Open 11pm–5.30am. The yachtie trappings at this Las Palmas outpost of the Pacha empire resemble those at the Playa del Inglés branch and – given the portside location – hint at the likely origins of many of its well-heeled clientele, which includes the occasional celebrity.

▲ THE CAMEL BAR

There's no *terraza*, so the emphasis is firmly on the dance floor, where the 35 to 50-plus crowd gets down to salsa and disco. There's no cover charge but drinks are expensive and you'll need smart casual dress to get in the door.

Lesbian & gay bars and clubs

Bridge Club Iron

C/Mariana Pineda 17. Daily 10pm–3am. Giant, blown-up pics of Hollywood stars looking rough decorate the monochrome interior of *Bridge Club Iron*, the most convivial of Las Palmas' gay bars. There's nothing rough, however, about the predominantly well-dressed, rather middle-class crowd of 30- and 40-something men and their heterosexual friends.

Miau

C/Martínez de Escobar 37. Daily 9pm–3am, later at weekends. Las Palmas' gay scene fights to compete with the siren call of the gay nightlife in the island's south by staying resolutely hispanic. The friendly and mostly local crowd at *Miau*, the liveliest gay club in the city, freaks out unashamedly to the infectious South American pop, and the best policy is simply to join in. Mostly gay male, but some lesbians and heteros too.

Live music

Auditorio Alfredo Kraus

Avda Príncipe de Asturias ☎ 928 491 773, ◍ www.auditorio-alfredokraus.com; box office 10am–2pm & 4.30–8.30pm ☎ 902 405 504. This magnificent concert hall, named after distinguished Las Palmas-born tenor Alfredo Kraus, opened in 1997 on a breathtaking site at the southern end of the Playa de las Canteras. In addition to being home to the Orquesta Filarmónica de Gran Canaria, it stages the Canary Islands' Music Festival (◍ www.festivaldecanarias. com) at the start of the year which regularly attracts conductors and performers of international standing. It is also one of the venues for the annual summer Jazz Festival (◍ www.canariasjazz.com) and the International Film festival in the spring (◍ www.festivalcine-laspalmas.com).

El Palacio Latino

C/Luis Morote 51. Open daily. The largest Cuban club in the city is an absolute must for any fan of latin music. The South Seas-style decor may not be to everyone's taste and the venue is a little faded, but the live salsa bands at this spacious venue are excellent, and the atmosphere is irresistible. From Monday to Thursday salsa lessons are available from 9.30–11.30pm; on Saturdays there's a daytime salsa session from 5am–11pm; Sundays are frequently given over to concerts. Drinks are at club prices.

▼ ALFRED KRAUS STATUE

Telde and around

With a population of around 100,000, big, bustling Telde is Gran Canaria's second city, with the commerce and heavy traffic to match its size and importance. There was already a settlement here in pre-Hispanic times, its ancient significance reflected by the major archeological sites of Cuatro Puertas and Poblado de Tufia, and in the many reproductions of the town's unofficial symbol, the Ídolo de Tara, a red pre-Hispanic fertility sculpture now exhibited in the Museo Canario in Las Palmas. Though its fringes are sprawling and industrial, at its heart Telde has three distinct historic neighbourhoods, the *barrios* of San Juan, San Francisco and San Gregorio, each with its own character and all rewarding to explore. Locals are also justifiably proud of the municipality's coastline and its wide variety of beaches, from the broad, urban strand at Melenara to the low-key charms of Agua Dulce or Ojos de Garza. They're all the haunt of locals rather than visitors. Inland, the land to the west climbs steeply to the lush Barranco de los Cernícalos, a beautiful spot for a walk and one of the few places on the island where you can see flowing water all year round. The upland town of Valsequillo, most easily reached from Telde, stands in a very scenic setting that is particularly beautiful at almond blossom time in February.

San Juan

Telde's grandest and most architecturally distinguished *barrio* is the so-called *zona fundacional* (foundation area) of San Juan. It's one of the most extensive historic districts in Gran Canaria, with streets of graceful colonial houses, not perhaps as grand as those of Vegueta in Las Palmas but just as dignified, and equally enjoyable to explore. At its heart is the fine set-piece of the **Plaza de San Juan Bautista**, fringed by the main civil and religious buildings, including the *ayuntamiento* (town hall), and the

---

Visiting Telde

Arriving in Telde from the motorway, the main historic districts are laid out either side of the park of San Gregorio and the wide, straight Avenida del Cabildo Insular; the pedestrian promenade down the centre of the avenue is known as the Rambla de San Gregorio. Telde's **tourist information office** is in a single-storey colonial house in San Juan at C/León y Castillo 2 (Mon–Fri 8am–3pm; ☎828 013 312, ⊛www.ayuntamientodetelde.org).

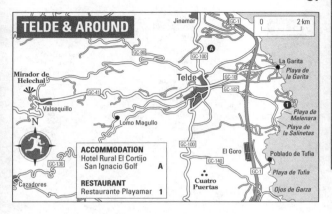

Basilica Menor de San Juan Bautista (daily 9am–12.30pm & 5–8pm), which dates from the town's foundation in the late fourteenth century and whose eclectic art and architecture reflect its long history. The church's sixteenth-century Gothic portal is flanked by two early twentieth-century towers; inside, there's a splendid early sixteenth-century Flemish Gothic altar, which is framed by a later, eighteenth-century altar. The image of Christ on the cross came from the Americas and was made from corn paste using a technique developed by the indigenous people of Michoacán in Mexico. The figures of San Pedro Mártir de Verona and of San Juan Evangelista date from the end of the eighteenth century and the beginning of the nineteenth, and are by the notable Canarian sculptor José Lujan Pérez.

There's an appealing little children's park with a small aviary close to the basilica on C/Licenciado Calderín, while northwest of the plaza, on C/Juan Carlos I, the seventeenth-century Renaissance church of

San Pedro Mártir de Verona is used for art exhibitions (daily 8am–3pm & 5–9pm; free). Telde's most important museum lies a few hundred metres south along C/León y Castillo. The **Museo de León y Castillo** (Mon–Fri 8am–8pm, Sat 10am–8pm, Sun 10am–1pm; ☎928 691 377; free), grouped around a couple of lovely patios with galleried wooden balconies, was the birthplace of Telde's two most famous sons, Fernando and Juan de León y Castillo and is a typical Canario house of the colonial era in Mudéjar style. Fernando, a politician and diplomat, rose to be a minister in the Spanish government and ambassador to France during the nineteenth century, and the bulk of the displays reflect his glittering career, with the case that held his ambassadorial credentials and a splendid Sèvres et Limoges table centrepiece. Rather less glamorously, Juan was an engineer who drew up the plans for the magnificent harbour of Puerto de la Luz in Las Palmas – a legacy that is arguably more enduring than

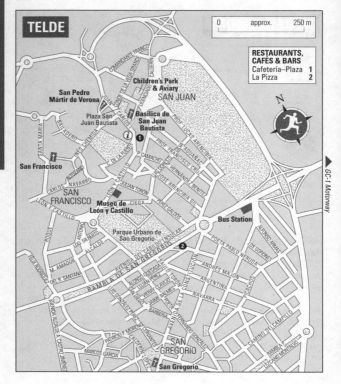

that of any politician. There's an English language leaflet available at reception.

San Francisco

Close to the tourist office at the foot of C/León y Castillo, the peaceful lane of Inés Chemida leads to the *barrio* of San Francisco, the most beguiling part of Telde. A huddle of simple, mostly single-storey whitewashed houses and secret gardens with bougainvillea tumbling over the walls, its winding streets and sleepy plazas have a distinctly rural feel; the steep C/Altozano is particularly picturesque. From the further of the two plazas in front of the church of San Francisco it's possible to look out across the valley over orange groves and banana plantations. The church itself is usually locked.

San Gregorio

Telde's third historic *barrio* is also the main commercial heart of Telde and, during the day, the most animated district in town. Though it lacks the lost-in-time feel of San Juan or San Francisco, the imposing Neoclassical church of San Gregorio is worth a look. Designed by Diego Nicolás Eduardo – who also designed

▲ BARRIO SAN FRANCISCO

the church at Agüimes – it has outstanding altarpieces by Arencibia Gil, an image of San Gregorio Taumaturgo by José Lujan Pérez and a nineteenth-century carving of the Virgin of Dolores by Silvestre Bello. The little plaza in front of the church is attractive, and in the streets around it isolated colonial houses survive among the more modern development.

Playa de Melenara

4km east of Telde; hourly white bus (no number) from Rambla de San Gregorio in central Telde. By car take the GC-102 road from central Telde; Melenara is east of the autopista and well signposted. Backed by an attractive traffic-free promenade and with a good choice of restaurants on the seafront offering Canarian cuisine and fresh seafood, the broad beach of Playa de Melenara is the most impressive of Telde's urban beaches. The 600-metre curve of fine, dark basaltic sand is looked over from an offshore rock by a bronze statue of Neptune, the Atlantic rollers crashing at his feet. The British privateer and explorer Sir Francis Drake landed here in 1595 while attacking the island, but was repulsed by local herdsmen; though Melenara remains very much a locals' beach, the welcome to visitors is these days a good deal warmer.

The northern beaches

North of Melenara, and beyond the imposing, if bland, Instituto Canario de Ciencas Marinas (not open to the public), modern suburban housing spreads along the coast to the breezy Playa del Hombre – popular with surfers and bodyboarders but devoid of facilities – and on to the dark sandy Hoya del Pozo, which is the most sheltered beach in these parts and therefore the best for a swim. Even further on is the more developed Playa de la Garita, another dark volcanic sand beach which has several restaurants and a couple of defensive bunkers dating from World War II, as well as a surfing and bodyboarding zone. A broad, well-made footpath follows the rocky coast; from Melenara to La Garita it's about 3km.

Playa de Salinetas

Easily reached on foot along the coast south of Playa de Melenara is Playa de Salinetas, a sandy cove where the houses open directly onto the beach, with numerous pathways between them offering access to the sands. This is the

▲ PLAYA TUFIA

traditional summer resort of the families of Telde; today it's used among others by surfers and bodyboarders. It's also a popular residential area, with considerable new development inland from the beach.

Poblado de Tufia

6km southeast of Telde; exit GC-1 motorway at El Goro industrial zone; no public transport. Daily 8am–8pm. Free. Straddling a narrow headland at the entrance to the fishing settlement of Punta de Silva is the Poblado de Tufia, one of the largest pre-Hispanic archeological sites on the island, with caves and rough stone houses in two principal clusters. Its windswept location on a tiny headland, no more than a couple of hundred metres wide at its narrowest, is undeniably dramatic, though unfortunately the site is fenced off and sometimes locked. It overlooks two small beaches: to the north, the small, sheltered golden sandy cove of Agua Dulce (literally "sweet water"), where the sea is exceptionally clear; it's a good spot for diving. To the south, the at times rather wild and windy sandy beach of **Playa de Tufia** lies at the foot of a low, rocky cliff into which fishermen built their cave dwellings – some of which have

been reoccupied recently. The owners' fishing boats are moored in the bay, and offshore there's more good diving.

Ojos de Garza

2km south of Tufia; take airport exit from GC-1, follow signs for Base Aerea then bear left. Bus #19 or #36 from Telde bus station. Ojos de Garza is a tiny settlement made up of a single row of whitewashed fishermen's houses fronting the wide pebble and sand beach – when the surf is up here, the sea can seem dramatically close. It's a very low-key place, with few facilities other than a single café, but in an island so single-mindedly geared to tourism its lack of development is appealing. The coast here is rich in bird life and sea urchins, while the Roque de Gando (Rock of Gando) forms a major coastal feature here.

Cuatro Puertas

6km south of Telde on GC-100, signposted from the main road. Global bus #35 from Telde. Mon–Fri 8am–8pm. Free. The stark red mountain of Montaña Bermeja was a sacred site to the ancient Canarios, and the Cuatro Puertas complex remains one of the most atmospheric pre-Hispanic sites on the island, thanks to its superbly scenic location as much as for the undeniably impressive remains. On the crest of the hill stands an *almogaren* – a site for rituals during which priests made offerings to earn the favour of the gods. A series of artificially excavated channels and bowls in the rock here would have been filled with milk and other liquids as part of the ceremony. The site takes its name – "four doors" – from the four square carved entrances to a large cave to the right of the entrance to the complex. The cave's purpose is unclear, though it's not thought to have been a living area. Across the crest of the hill the cave dwellings of Los Pilares are intriguing to explore, though note that despite a retaining wall and rope handrail it's occasionally steep here and it can be a bit of a scramble to reach the furthest caves. Outside the Cueva de los Papeles you can still see the holes for door posts and a drinking trough; inside, the carved triangles for which it is known – thought to be fertility symbols – are rather indistinct.

Barranco de los Cernícalos

Lomo Magullo, 6km west of Telde on a minor road or via the GC-130, turning right at La Colomba. From the village of Lomo Magullo a marked path ascends the lush, well-watered valley of the Barranco de los Cernícalos to a series of beautiful year-round waterfalls – a real rarity on Gran Canaria. A comfortable walk lasting 2–3 hours takes you from the reed-covered valley floor to the deep cleft that forms the main falls. The path follows the watercourse through a wood of willow trees, with panoramas of the dense broom and wild olives that cloak the sides of the valley; in winter in particular when the rainfall is higher the valley bottom can be a vivid green. Most of the route is only moderately difficult, but you should take care on some stretches where there's a danger of slipping in the wet along the riverbed and on the cliffs, or if attempting to climb the falls. Wear proper walking boots and be aware that in periods of sustained wet weather the water-course becomes a fully fledged river and the path is sometimes entirely impassable.

Valsequillo

10km west of Telde on GC-41. Bus #13 or #43 from Plaza San Juan, Telde. In a lush, hilly setting high above Telde and reached through orange groves and posh suburbia, the little town of Valsequillo has a tiny historic core clustered around the large, early twentieth-century church of San Miguel, with a couple of basic café-bars for refreshment. The main reason for coming here, however, is the town's lovely setting in an eroded caldera. This is an exceptionally

▲ BARRANCO DE LOS CERNÍCALOS

beautiful part of the island, especially in February when Valsequillo, together with its neighbours Tenteniguada, Las Vegas and La Barrera link up to run a festival celebrating the ruta de almendro en flor (see p.177) and the green hills are enlivened by beautiful almond blossom. During the festival the roads hereabouts are packed with locals moving from town to town, and each village has its stalls selling local food and drink at the side of the road with perhaps a goat or two roasting slowly over a fire. High above Valsequillo, a well-surfaced road spirals up to the Mirador de Helechal viewpoint, from where there's a superb view of deep green valleys and terraced hillsides. The road to the mirador is signposted and exits the main road by a petrol station before you reach the town centre, circling the residential outskirts before emerging above the old town.

Hotels

Hotel Rural El Cortijo San Ignacio Golf

GC-1 motorway km 6.4, El Cortijo exit ☎928 712 427, @www.cortijosanig-naciogolf.com. Surrounded by an 18-hole golf course, this lovely small hotel, north of Telde, has just sixteen double and two single rooms. It occupies a beautiful whitewashed eighteenth-century farmhouse, tucked behind high walls and with its public rooms furnished elegantly in country house style. The exposed beams, stonework and galleried wooden balconies add to the atmosphere. There's a very attractive pool area. Rooms are simple and tasteful, with iron beds and wooden furniture,

and only the looming presence across the valley of the ugly suburb of Jimamar dents the air of blissful repose. €90.

Cafes, restaurants and bars

Cafetería–Plaza

C/León y Castillo 7, San Juan, Telde. Spacious café–bar, handily located just across from the tourist office, is a pleasant spot for a cheap, light lunch – tortilla española with a roll and alioli (garlic mayonnaise) will set you back less than €2.

La Pizza

Avda Cabildo Insular 2, San Gregorio, Telde ☎928 682 834. Daily 1.30–4pm & 8pm–midnight, Fri & Sat till 2am. Large pizza and pasta restaurant on the fringe of the Rambla de San Gregorio in the centre of Telde. Pizza size is generous, the salads are big and the tortelloni in a cream and mushroom sauce is very good. Prices start around the €5 mark.

Restaurante Playamar

C/Luis Morote 45, Melenara ☎928 133 007. Mon, Wed, Thurs & Sun noon–midnight, Fri & Sat noon–1am, closed Tues. Wonderful, thick, dhal-like gofio escaldado with red onion, fresh mint and green mojo makes an excellent and filling start to a meal at this beachfront restaurant, and the papas arrugadas are tip-top too. Starter portions are big enough for two to share, while the fresh fish is simple but good. Mains cost around €7. For the best views over the beach and the Neptune statue offshore, try to bag a table in the upstairs dining room.

The east coast

The east of Gran Canaria is the first part of the island many visitors see on their journey south from the airport, but the industrial zones, modern urban sprawl and wind farms to either side of the GC-1 motorway scarcely suggest a holiday paradise, with only the mountains to the west and the shimmering Atlantic to the east hinting at the region's extensive charms. Once away from the motorway, in the beautiful valley of the Barranco de Guayadeque, in the historic towns of Agüimes and Ingenio, or in the numerous small coastal villages and beaches you'll find the real key to the area's appeal. For active visitors, this stretch of coast has the island's best windsurfing and some of its best diving, along with some wonderful scenery for nature lovers and walkers, while for foodies the little towns of Arinaga or Castillo del Romeral are as good a place as any to enjoy the simple Canario pleasure of fresh fish, grilled straight from the sea.

Ingenio

Ingenio sprawls uphill eastwards along the northern side of the Barranco de Guayadeque, from the largely modern district of Carrizal alongside the GC-1 motorway to the original town of Ingenio itself, where most points of interest are concentrated. The old town clusters around the spacious, attractive Plaza de la Candelaria, dominated by the twin towers and dome of the Iglesia de la Candelaria, which dates from 1901 and contains a Gothic altar, though sadly you'll probably find it locked unless there's a service on. The narrow, winding old streets on the north side of the church make for pleasant strolling. Ingenio is well known for its handicrafts industries, particularly its open-weave tablecloths, which make pricey if authentic souvenirs of a trip to the island. To the east of the old town, at C/ Pascual Richart 2, the **Casa de Postas** (Mon–Fri 9am–8pm)

Visiting the east coast

The east of the island is well served by Global's bus network (⌨www.globalsu.net), with **buses** from Las Palmas to Ingenio and Agüimes (#11 & #21) and Castillo del Romeral (#8), and Arinaga served by buses from Agüimes (#22) and Maspalomas (#25). Bus #35 links Agüimes with Ingenio and Telde every two hours. The two main towns both have **a tourist office**: Ingenio's is west of the old town, just off the GC-100 road in the Casa de Postas, C/Pascual Richart 2 (Mon–Fri 9am–8pm); ☎928 783 799, ⌨www.villadeingenio.org); the one in Agüimes is in the Centro de Interpretación del Casco Histórico on Plaza de San Antonio Abad (Mon–Fri 9am–3pm, Sat & Sun 9am–2pm, closes one hour earlier in summer; ☎928 124 183, ⌨www.aguimes.es).

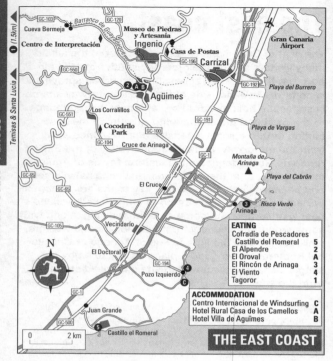

Temisas & Santa Lucía ◄

❶ (1.5km) ◄

EATING

Cofradía de Pescadores	
Castillo del Romeral	5
El Alpendre	2
El Oroval	A
El Rincón de Arinaga	3
El Viento	4
Tagoror	1

ACCOMMODATION

Centro Internacional de Windsurfing	C
Hotel Rural Casa de los Camellos	A
Hotel Villa de Agüimes	B

THE EAST COAST

is an attractive gallery complex grouped around a traditional patio; it provides a venue for changing exhibitions by local artists and also houses the town's tourist information office. Ingenio was a centre of the island's sugar industry, which boomed during the sixteenth century before being ruined by competition from the Americas – the name Ingenio means sugar mill and an example decorates a roundabout on the road between the town centre and the district of Carrizal. North of the crossroads in the centre of Ingenio on C/Camino Real de Gando stands the **Museo de Piedras y Artesanía Canaria de Ingenio** (Mon–Sat 8am–

6.30pm; free). This Museum of Rocks and Crafts contains, as the name suggests, a small collection of quartz, minerals and glass, but really the place is an oddball, if likeable, miscellany. They sell the characteristic local open-weave cloth here, plus locally sourced aloe vera products, cigars and flower perfumes. There's also a chapel, some noisy parrots and hens on the patio outside, and a café and bar.

Playa del Burrero

Incongruously tucked under the final approach to the airport, Ingenio's windy main beach, Playa del Burrero, is a windsurfers' and locals' haunt,

▲ BARRANCO DE GUAYADEQUE

where the roar of the surf mixes with the roar of the planes. The beach's fine sand and shingle is backed by a smart new promenade and some attractive residential development, and a few fishing boats still pull up at the northern end of the sand. Quite the oddest place to bathe in Gran Canaria, however, is surely the little beach of San Agustín just to the north, nestling at the foot of a low cliff and with the airport perimeter fence slicing across it.

Barranco de Guayadeque

Signposted from GC-100 road in Aguïmes. The highly scenic Barranco de Guayadeque is one of the most archeologically and ecologically important ravines on the island. Cutting up from the coast to pass between the towns of Ingenio and Aguïmes before slicing deep into the rugged interior of the island, it shelters within its boundaries a couple of plant species that don't grow anywhere else, along with fascinating remnants of the pre-Hispanic islanders' cave dwelling past. At the top of the ravine, its rocks are composed of relatively young volcanic material less than 300,000 years old, but down at sea level the geology dates back 14 million years. Halfway up the valley the cave village of **Cueva Bermeja**, with its chapel carved out of the rock and whitewashed house fronts opening onto cave dwellings that are still inhabited, still holds on though in general the human population of the *barranco* is dwindling, down from 450 in 1970 to just 172 at the end of the century. Cueva Bermeja is a reliable and photogenic pitstop for camera-clicking bus tours, but to make sense of this stunning landscape it's a good idea to visit the Centro de Interpretación at the valley entrance first (see p.90). The *barranco* is a mass of flowering plants, and particularly lush and green in the late winter, when the almond trees are in blossom higher up the valley. It's a paradise for walkers: several **footpaths** of varying difficulties are marked on a map issued by the tourist office in Ingenio, including a couple which reach as far inland as the volcanic crater of Caldera de los Marteles.

Centro de Interpretación de Guayadeque

Tues–Sat 9am–5pm, Sun 10am–6pm. €2.40. The stylish modernist front of this impressive museum conceals a cave network that burrows into the side of the *barranco* and houses the exhibition space. Particularly engrossing are the sections explaining how the scrubby vegetation of the semi-arid coast gradually changes into the lushness of the ravine's higher reaches. The section on the indigenous Canarios describes the various prehistoric sites scattered around the *barranco* – including the Cueva de Morros de Avila with its geometric paintings, and the funeral caves of Puntón del Guirre or Cuevas de la Bota which are, characteristically, on the shady side of the valley. The indigenous peoples carved their cave dwellings in the valley sides of Guayadeque because the rock was soft but resistant, and so

easy to excavate but unlikely to collapse. A mummy, found in the nineteenth century in a cave in Guayadeque, lends an enjoyably spooky note for children, and there's an enlightening section on the agriculture and diet of the original inhabitants which suggests that, if not quite an earthly paradise, pre-Hispanic Gran Canaria was a healthy and bountiful land.

Agüimes

Neat, pleasant Agüimes is one of the most interesting towns in the east of the island, set in an open landscape of volcanic hills that are carpeted in winter with brilliant vegetation, including succulents and flowering shrubs. The best views of the town and its domed church are from the road to Santa Lucia or from the Barranco de Guayadeque that separates the town from its northern neighbour, Ingenio. Agüimes has an attractive, compact *casco histórico* clustered around the imposing domed Neoclassical church of San Sebastián, designed by Diego Nicolás Eduardo, consecrated in 1808 and regarded as one of the best examples of Canario classicism. Sadly it's usually locked unless there's a service on. The town was the seat of a bishopric from 1486 until 1837 – a time when much church property on the island was being sold off – which explains the splendour of the church compared to the simplicity of the rest of Agüimes. The town predates the Spanish, though pretty much everything you now see dates from after the 1478 conquest. In contrast to towns in the north of the island, where agricultural prosperity led to more elaborate architecture, most of Agüimes' houses are

▼ CENTRO DE INTERPRETACIÓN

quite humble, single storey affairs, reflecting the relative poverty of the district, which led to large-scale emigration to Cuba, Puerto Rico and elsewhere. Beautifully maintained thanks to the *ayuntamiento*, some of the larger houses have been put to institutional

▲ AGÜIMES

use: of these, the **Casa de Mujer** (Women's Centre) on C/Sol is perhaps the most attractive, with a typical wooden galleried patio that is well worth a look if the door is open. To gain a better understanding of the town's history and growth head for Plaza de San Antonio Abad and the excellent **Centro de Interpretación del Casco Historico** (Mon–Fri 9am–3pm, Sat & Sun 9am–2pm, closes one hour earlier in summer; free), where an absorbing little exhibition traces the development of Agüimes over the last thousand years, explaining the building styles, furnishings and materials of the area, such as the *tejas de muslo* – red clay roof tiles formed by the tiler using his own thigh (*muslo*) as a mould. Agüimes' cultural heritage isn't limited to its old buildings; it's also a traditional centre of Canario *lucha* wrestling, and has one of the liveliest carnival traditions on the island (see p.177).

Cocodrilo Park

Los Corralillos km 5.5, Agüimes ☎928 784 725; bus Tues, Thurs & Sun 10am

from Faro de Maspalomas. Daily except Sat 10am–5pm. €9.90, €6.90 children. With not just crocodiles but birds, tigers, chimpanzees and snakes, Cocodrilo Park is no mere menagerie but a zoo with a purpose: it provides a home for exotic animals that have been impounded by customs or abandoned or mistreated by owners. The park was opened in 1988 as a private venture by the Balser family and receives no government subsidy for its work. Some of the animals brought here have been badly mistreated and it takes time for the park staff to nurse them back to health; others, including the Bengal tigers, have been bred at Cocodrilo Park itself. The quickest approach by car is not from Agüimes itself but on the direct GC-104 road from Cruce de Arinaga.

Playa de Vargas

Reached via a long side road exiting the GC-191 at Montaña los Vélez between Cruce de Arinaga and Carrizal, the Playa de Vargas is a long, stoney beach that offers some of the best windsurfing conditions on the

▲ ARINAGA

island. There are no real facilities – except plenty of parking spaces – and windsurfers should bring their own boards if they want to enjoy the windy conditions and rough surf.

Arinaga

The pleasant little coastal town of Arinaga is a popular weekend destination for locals and a very pleasant spot for a lazy dip and a long seafood lunch. It's a place of no real architectural distinction, but it does have a smart and attractive seafront promenade and an inviting cluster of restaurants close to the jetty, and the rock and dark sand beach has some naturally sheltered sections that are perfect for swimming in the clear water. There are still-working salt pans – remnants of a traditional island industry – immediately to the south of the town, and some preserved lime kilns on the seafront at Risco Verde on the northern outskirts.

Playa del Cabrón

Immediately north of Arinaga, reached via a rutted track between the volcanic cone of Montaña de Arinaga and the lighthouse at Punta de Arinaga, the sandy little cove of the Playa del Cabrón comes as an unexpected pleasure. It has no facilities as such but does possess a low-key charm, enhanced by the surrounding cliffs eroded into weird shapes, the few whitewashed houses and a view that extends to the islet of El Roque offshore. The real draw, however, is the Marine Reserve of Arinaga which offers some of the island's best diving – it's here that many of the commercial diving operators (see p.175) will bring you. There's a spectacular array of marine life plus an underwater volcanic landscape of arches, swim-throughs, caves and overhangs.

Pozo Izquierdo

Bus #1 from Puerto de Mogán and Puerto Rico or #5 from Maspalomas and Playa del Inglés then (infrequent) #17 from El Doctoral. The futuristic wind turbines that surround the small coastal village of Pozo Izquierdo hint at the reason for the area's fame, for this section of the east coast is the best location for windsurfing in the whole of Gran Canaria. Excellent conditions prevail between March and September (July and August are the very best months) and a windsurfing school (Centro Internacional de Windsurfing ☎928 121 400, ✆www.pozo-ciw.com), separated by a stretch of modern promenade from the village, offers courses from beginner to advanced level – the exact location for your practice depends on your ability. Pozo Izquierdo itself is not an especially interesting village architecturally, though the promenade is attractively laid out with windsurfing motifs set into the paving, and the small, dark sand beach, protected from the rough sea by a breakwater, is appealing enough. The flat country behind the village is given over to the cultivation of bananas and tomatoes in vast, makeshift plastic greenhouses.

Juan Grande

Bus #1 from Puerto de Mogán and Puerto Rico and #5 from Maspalomas and Playa del Inglés. The eye-catching whitewashed chapel and house complex of the family of the Conde de la Vega Grande – important landowners in this part of the island – is an arresting sight at the side of the GC-500 road in the hamlet of Juan Grande. The colonial buildings are noteworthy for their size and beauty in a part of the island that in post-conquest times was thinly settled and largely devoid of major architectural landmarks. The chapel of **Nuestra Señora de Guadalupe** here has beautiful engravings and an image of the Virgin of Guadalupe that was brought from Mexico in the sixteenth century – unfortunately the chapel is usually locked due to ongoing refurbishment work. The chapel is set back from the road on a simple plaza, while the wide, low house sits behind a rough whitewashed wall with a crucifix above the gate.

Castillo del Romeral

A traditional centre of the island's salt industry, the village of Castillo del Romeral is best known today for its seafront

▲ WINDSURFER STATUE

fishermen's cooperative restaurant, right next to the jetty where the boats pull up. The village has a lovely sandy beach, which is backed by date palms and a long row of single-storey whitewashed houses but, like many spots on the east coast, it's still relatively undisturbed by the tourist industry, and there are few facilities. The village takes its name from the fortress which once stood here to protect the saltpans.

Shops

Centro Comercial Atlántico

Avda del Atlántico 359, Vecindario; Global bus #66 or 69 from Las Palmas or Maspalomas. The most important retail centre in the south of the island, the slick, modern CC Atlántico contains a Carrefour hypermarket plus many well-known Spanish and international fashion names including Zara, Cortefiel and Mango.

Hotels

Casa de los Camellos

C/Progreso 12, Aguïmes ☎928 785 003, ⊛www.hecansa.com. The startling bronze of a recumbent camel outside means there's no missing this former inn and camel stable in the heart of Aguïmes. Now a charming small hotel where the staff are the students and tutors of the Hecansa hotel school, guest rooms are grouped around a patio with lush subtropical planting; those on the upper levels are reached by outside stairs and traditional wooden galleries. All rooms are comfortably and traditionally furnished and are en suite. There's a pleasant restaurant too, *El Oroval*. €70.

Villa de Aguïmes

C/Sol 3, Aguïmes ☎928 785 003, ⊛www.hecansa.com. Located in the former town hall, a 200-year old house with galleried balconies and whitewashed walls, the atmospheric *Villa de Aguïmes* has just six rooms, furnished with a mix of antiques and traditional wooden furniture produced by the students of the local carpentry school. There's no restaurant: guests take their meals at the *Casa de los Camellos*, the *Villa de Aguïmes'* sister hotel. The rooms, which are all en-suite, represent very good value for money. €63.

Hostel

Centro Internacional de Windsurfing

Pozo Izquierdo ☎928 121 400, ⊛www.pozo-ciw.com. Clean, bright modern accommodation in eight-bed dorms at the windsurfing centre in Pozo Izquierdo comes complete with direct sea views, a gym and outdoor pool, and Internet facilities. There's a restaurant and bar too. €20 per person.

Cafés, restaurants and bars

Cofradía de Pescadores Castillo del Romeral

Avda de la Playa, Castillo del Romeral ☎928 728 199. Mon–Sat until 11pm, Sun until 6pm. Cheerful (and popular) fish restaurant run by the village fishermen's co-operative, where if you grab a seat outside you can see the boats on the beach in front of you that caught the fish on your plate. It's extremely busy – be prepared to queue – but staff are efficient and friendly and it's an experience worth waiting for.

El Alpendre

C/Joaquin Artiles, Agüimes ☎928 124 400. Daily except Wed noon–midnight. Informal, lively bar/restaurant in a huddle of traditional buildings on the edge of Agüimes. Mains cost around €9 and the emphasis is on grilled meats, though with *papas arrugadas*, *pimientos de padrón* and *tortilla española* on the menu there's something for veggies too. There are a few Canary Island bottles on the wine list, and a wide terrace and lawn with children's swings to keep any kids entertained while you sup.

El Oroval

Hotel Rural Casa de los Camellos, C/ Progreso 12, Agüimes ☎928 785 003. Tues–Sun 8.30–10.30am, 1–4pm & 8–10pm. Charming, high-roofed traditional dining room in the hotel school in the old town in Agüimes. A meal here might start with delicious *almogrote* – a paste of peppers, cheese, tomato and garlic – before progressing to superb fresh fish simply grilled, or a more elaborate dish such as *ropa vieja* with octopus, beans and potatoes. Mains start at €7.

El Rincón de Arinaga

C/Alcalá Galiano 2, Arinaga ☎928 188 956. Daily except Wed 11am–midnight. *Piquillo* peppers stuffed with cod or *queso frito* (fried cheese) are among the specialities at this popular seafront restaurant opposite the *muelle* in Arinaga, and the fresh swordfish is a good bet too. Prices hover around the €10 mark and portions are generous.

El Viento

Avda Punta Tenefe 2, Pozo Izquierdo ☎928 121 052. Daily 11am–midnight. Big, slick bar-restaurant with an enviable, sunny position right on the seafront at Pozo Izquierdo, close to the Windsurfing Centre. There are reasonably priced pizzas – from €7 – and pasta selections including a few unusual sauces, such as rocket with taleggio cheese. The menu also offers focaccia sandwiches, steaks and fish, and there's no shortage of sea views to enjoy from the big windows while you eat. There's also a pool table.

▲ COFRADÍA DE PESCADORES

PLACES The east coast

▲ TAGOROR

Tagoror

Montaña las Tierras, Barranco de Guayadeque ☎928 172 013. Daily 10am–midnight. **High in the Barranco de Guayadeque, this celebrated cave restaurant is hollowed deep into the mountainside and attracts hordes of visitors as much for its novelty value as for the genuine Canario food, which is extremely good and reasonably priced.** If you prefer sun to subterranean gloom, the views from the sunny outside terrace are particularly lovely in February when the valley is lush and green and there's blossom everywhere, though note it can get chilly up here. At weekends they dish up more elaborate traditional favourites including *ropa vieja* and *sancocho* for around €6.

The Cumbre

Unspoiled, thinly populated and majestic, Gran Canaria's mountainous interior – known as the Cumbre or summit – is one of the delights of a visit to the island. The rugged *barrancos*, vast volcanic calderas, peaceful pine forests and cool mountain reservoirs here make the area a little paradise, criss-crossed by hiking trails and dotted with picnic spots, and particularly lovely in early spring when almond blossom brings the hillsides to life. It was the pristine ecosystems of these high mountains – rising to just under 2000m at Pozo de las Nieves, the highest point on the island – that were the main reason behind UNESCO's declaring Gran Canaria a World Biosphere Reserve in 2005. Scenery aside, the towns and villages of the interior may be small and sleepy, but are worth visiting for a taste of Canarian life almost unaltered by tourism. A marked trail, the Ruta Centro de las Cumbres, links some of the most spectacular landscape features, while watching over everything is the great basalt sentinel of Roque Nublo ("cloud rock"), the widely recognized symbol of this stunning region. Rugged it may be, but the Cumbre couldn't be easier to access, at least if you have your own transport: roads are mostly well surfaced – if twisting – and rarely busy.

Arteara

Set in a luxuriant date palm grove, Arteara is little more than a hamlet on the dramatic Playa del Inglés-San Bartolomé road, but its dramatic setting beneath the rugged walls of a *barranco* is a first taste of the scenic grandeur of the island's interior. Many visitors come here for the camel safaris, offered by either **Manolo's Camel Safari** (Barranco de Arteara 5–7 ☎928 798 686; €9 for 20min) at the entrance to the village, or **Camel Safari Park La Baranda** (C/La Baranda, Ruta de Fataga ☎928 798 680; €15 for 30min, €22 for 1hr), a little north of Arteara in the direction of Fataga. However, it's for a taste of pre-Hispanic civilization that Arteara is most memorable and for tangible evidence of this past, follow the single-track road that leads south through the village to the atmospheric **Parque Arqueológico de Arteara** (open access) on the site of a Canario necropolis. What at first appears to be just a field of rubble soon becomes quite obviously an elaborate archeological site as you follow the well-marked, if at times rough, path through the remains. The tombs were built from the debris of a natural rockslide – which is why they appear to grow out of the ground

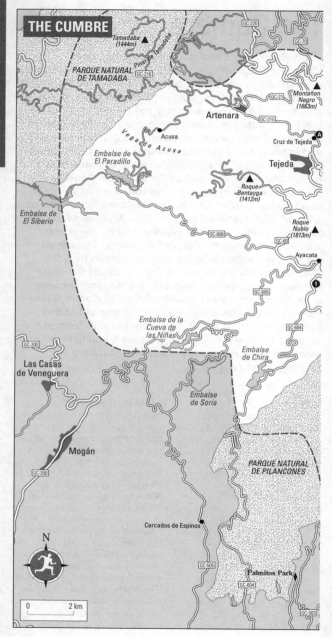

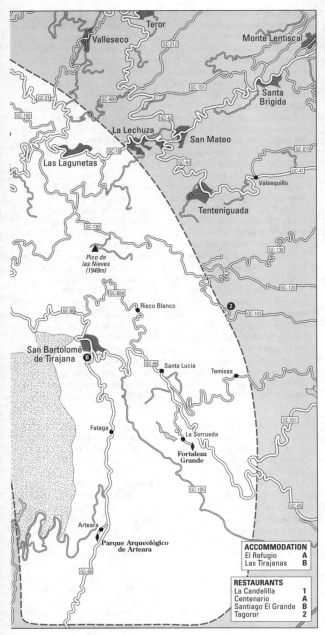

ACCOMMODATION

| El Refugio | A |
| Las Tirajanas | B |

RESTAURANTS

La Candelilla	1
Centenario	A
Santiago El Grande	B
Tagoror	2

Visiting the Cumbre

Global **bus** #18 (⊕ www.globalsu.net) is the most useful service for accessing the area by public transport, connecting the Faro de Maspalomas with San Bartolomé de Tirajana around six times daily, continuing on to Tejeda around four times a day. Route #34 links El Doctoral and Aguïmes with Temisas, Santa Lucía and San Bartolomé about eight times daily, less often at weekends. Bus #220 leaves Teror for Artenara on the hour during the day. With **your own transport** a 4WD vehicle is best for exploring off the beaten track. **From the north**, the GC-100 runs from Las Palmas as far as Monte Lentiscal, where the route passes through Santa Brigida and Vega de San Mateo, from which the GC-15 continues to Cruz de Tejeda. **From the east** the fastest access is via the Telde-Valsequillo road, the GC-41. **From the south** the GC-60 Playa del Inglés-Fataga road is direct if occasionally narrow and the GC-505 from El Pajar near Arguineguín is good for much of its length, deteriorating only beyond the turnoff for Soria. Only **from the west** is access a problem, though a well-surfaced but twisting single track road runs from San Nicolás de Tolentino to Vega de Acusa and Artenara, popular for its spectacular scenery but hard work for the driver. Alternatively, in the northwest the GC-220 ascends from the GC-2 motorway towards Artenara and Cruz de Tejeda through lovely pastoral scenery. This area is also hugely popular with both **bikers** and **cyclists** – the roads are well surfaced and relatively quiet, though if you're intending to cycle here you'll need to be fit and prepared for the combination of strong sun, summer heat, high altitude and steep inclines. **Tourist information** offices can be found in most of the larger villages. Artenara's is in the Centro de Recuperación de Artesanía (Mon–Fri 9.15am–3pm, Sat 10.15am–2.30pm; ⊕928 666 102), a little way down from the main square in the direction of Tamadaba. Tejeda's is in the Abraham Cárdenes sculpture museum on C/Leocadio Cabrera (Tues–Fri 11am–3.30pm, Sat 11.30am–2.30pm, Sun 11.20am–4pm; ⊕928 666 189, ⊕www.tejeda.es). Santa Lucía's office is in the busy commercial district of Vecindario, just off the GC-1 coast road (Plaza de la Era, Avda de Canarias, Vecindario ⊕928 125 260; Mon–Fri 8.30am–1.30pm & 4–6pm). San Bartolomé de Tirajana is part of the Maspalomas and Playa del Inglés municipality, and you should therefore enquire at one of the tourist offices on the coast. Tejeda's petrol station – it stands at the entrance to the village on the main road and is the only one for miles – is closed on Sundays.

– with the central nucleus of the site including a number of plundered tumuli, of which the most important is the Sepultura del Rey or King's Tomb. The sun's first rays fall directly on this tomb once a year on a certain day, while at the time of the autumn equinox in September there's another astronomical phenomenon known as the "double sun" when the sun appears to rise twice over the Amurga hills to the east of the site. Villagers once kept beehives in the necropolis, and on the death of the owner the hive would be destroyed and a black wreath placed atop it. A few abandoned examples can be seen on the way out of the complex.

Fataga

The approaches to Fataga are heralded by orange groves and date palms, the first signs that you're leaving the arid coast behind. It's a handy pit stop on the route into the centre of the island, with a petrol station and a couple of bars and restaurants on the main road through the village. There's also a bodega here, the *Bodega Tabaibilla* (Carreterra Fataga-

▲ FATAGA

Maspalomas km 1.2 ☎928 763 906; Mon–Sat 9am–5pm, Sun 9am–noon), reflecting the fact that Fataga is one of the more far-flung outposts of the island's wine industry and part of the *denominación de origen* Gran Canaria, producing good quality reds and whites using unusual grape varieties. Wine aside, the chief attraction is the village itself, a photogenic huddle of red-tiled roofs and whitewashed walls, very simple but fitting comfortably into the landscape. It comes alive for the annual Fiesta del Albaricoque (apricot festival) in the last week of April and first week of May.

San Bartolomé de Tirajana

Beyond Fataga, the road climbs out of the narrow *barranco* and enters the vast circular Caldera de Tirajana, a fertile agricultural oasis rimmed by mountains, with the island's highest peaks closing off the views to the north. It's in this area that the *guindilla* and *mejunje* fruit liqueurs that you may have tried in the island's restaurants are made, from cherries and oranges respectively and rum. San Bartolomé de Tirajana itself is a quiet town, tumbling over a hillside with superb

views of the surrounding landscape. There are a couple of atmospheric old lanes, some bars and a bodega, but the main focus is the simple church of **San Bartolomé de Tirajana**, consecrated in 1922 but with an eclectic collection of religious artefacts including a figure of St Bartholomew acquired in the eighteenth century and a rather creepy representation of Christ in a glass coffin. A new **Centro Rural** is being carved out of an old house opposite the church, comprising a hotel, *gofio* mill, bodega and Canarian

▲ SAN BARTOLOMÉ DE TIRAJANA

restaurant. High above the town at the entrance to the *Hotel Las Tirajanas*, a *mirador* offers excellent views towards the neighbouring town of Santa Lucía and the geological oddity of the **Risco Blanco** ("white cliff"). A little way to the south of the hotel, a hiking trail leads southwest out of town past the mesa-like outcrop of the Morros de las Vacas into the **Pinar de Pilancones**, a lush pine forest that forms part of the core of the UNESCO biosphere reserve. From here, keen walkers can continue across the mountains to Palmitos Park, a distance of some 8km or so – wear proper walking boots and a hat and carry water with you.

Risco Blanco

On the north side of Santa Lucía, at Rosiana, the minor GC-654 road signposted Taidia leads up through a lovely pastoral landscape and sleepy rural communities towards Risco Blanco, a cone-shaped chunk of mountainside that from a distance looks blindingly white, though its whiteness softens to golden yellow as you approach it. The sheer wall of Pozo de las Nieves – the highest point on the island – rears up in front of you as you approach Risco Blanco. This is a rewarding detour into a largely undiscovered corner of rural Gran Canaria, but note that the road is narrow and at times terrifyingly steep. It emerges onto the GC-60 just above San Bartolomé de Tirajana. The route is also popular with cyclists.

Santa Lucía

From San Bartolomé de Tirajana a road spirals down to the Barranco de Tirajana, where a bridge crosses the narrow stream bed before reaching Santa Lucía, neater and more self-consciously pretty than San Bartolomé. It's also a more established stop on the tourist circuit, not so much for its rather showy white-domed church, built in 1905, as for the **Museo Castillo de la Fortaleza** (daily 9am–5pm; €2) a tacky-looking but fascinating small museum on the road south of the village. The eclectic collection on the ground floor has everything from pre-Hispanic artefacts and specimens of indigenous butterflies and marine life to a rather glum military room watched over by a faded portrait of Franco. Far more appealing is the upstairs art gallery, with a small but diverse collection of abstract and representational art, including one by the Canarian-based Catalan painter Miró Mainou.

Santa Lucía's narrow, winding lanes have a quiet charm, particularly those behind the new *ayuntamiento*.

Embalse de La Sorrueda

Just south of Santa Lucía, the GC-651 – a side road off the GC-65 – brings you to the Embalse de La Sorrueda, one of the island's most photographed reservoirs. The lush palms at the side of the lake, the steep shoreline and the rocky island in the middle create a picturesque ensemble and for the best view head to the little *mirador*, reached down a short but bumpy track.

The Fortaleza de Ansite

The GC-651 road continues past the Embalse de La Sorrueda to the daunting citadel of the Fortaleza de Ansite (open access), a stern rock outcrop that was the last redoubt of the pre-Hispanic Canarios. In 1480, with the island almost entirely in Spanish hands, the Canarios retreated here only to be defeated four years later, on April 29, 1484; they leapt to their deaths from the fortress rather than be captured. From the rough parking space at the fortress a path leads along the steep and crumbling – but safe – eastern flank of the hill, at the far end of which a cave burrows clear through the mountain. It may look interesting but with the interior littered with ominously fresh-looking rock falls, it's best viewed from outside. To appreciate the remarkably fort-like qualities of the hill, retrace your steps to the GC-65 main road and continue in the direction of Vecindario. Stopping on this narrow and busy road is not always easy but the views are worth it if you can.

Temisas

Temisas, a wonderfully unspoiled village on the GC-550, sits in a wild and mountainous landscape, backed by cliff-like slopes and with the distinctive Roque Aguayro closing off the view to the sea. The hills above Temisas are full of pre-Hispanic caves and the village is the centre of the island's olive production, but there's very little to do here, other than enjoy the serenity. Still, if you want to see a Canarian village untouched by mass tourism, this is it.

Cruz Grande and the Embalse de Chira

At Cruz Grande, high above San Bartolomé de Tirajana, several well-marked and well-made paths fan out to explore the forested landscape: north

along an old *camino real* to the forests and picnic sites of Llanos del Garañon; south beyond San Bartolomé de Tirajana to the Degollada de la Manzanilla; and west along a ridge to the Embalse de Chira. This reservoir can also be reached by car by heading a little north of Cruz Grande to where a side road winds the 8km down to the lake, descending through sparse pine forest and through the scattered settlement of Cercados de Araña before reaching the lake and, finally, the dam. The reservoir is big and offers the unusual opportunity to see Roque Nublo and Pozo de las Nieves across a wide expanse of green water – walk part way across the dam for the best views – plus places to picnic at the reservoir's edge. From the side of the main road in Cercados de Araña a path continues to the larger reservoir of Soria.

PLACES The Cumbre

▲ TEMISAS

▲ ROQUE NUBLO

Ayacata and Roque Nublo

The village of Ayacata clings to a rock wall, watched over by **ominous massifs**. It's a surprisingly sheltered spot given the drama of its setting, and after the hard driving, cycling or walking involved in getting here, it's a great place to break for lunch, though such is the popularity of the restaurants you may have trouble parking. West of the village, a minor road descends to the reservoir of **Cueva de las Niñas**, with a lovely setting amid the pine forests of Pajonales, but the main reason for stopping at Ayacata is to make the ascent to **Roque Nublo**. This 64-metre, basalt monolith is visible from many points across the island's interior – its tip is 1813m above sea level – and can even be seen from as far away as the dunes of Maspalomas. The path up to the rock is, like many in the mountains, based on a restored *camino real* – one of the ancient mountain highways of the island – and is relatively easy, starting from La Goleta car park at La Goleta, just above Ayacata. The route follows a ridge at first before a short but steep section brings you up onto a wide, stoney tableland. Roque Nublo is at the far end of this plateau. All around are stunning views of the island's interior: to the north keep an eye out in particular for clouds – formed by the trade winds hitting the island's uplands – streaming down over the side of the Caldera de Tejeda like a snowy tablecloth. The rock itself was formed during the most recent major period of volcanic activity in this part of the island over three million years ago, and however slender it may seem from afar, it's pretty impressive up close. To descend, you have to retrace your steps towards La Goleta. If you want to explore this beautiful landscape at more length, a level path encircles the rock and another descends through cool pine forest to the village of La Culata. It's about a 35-minute walk up to Roque Nublo; the walk down rather less.

Roque Bentayga

From the Ayacata-Tejeda road a tortuous but fabulously scenic route with little in the way of crash barriers spirals up to Roque Bentayga, another imposing volcanic rock soaring to 1412m above sea level in the centre of the Cuenca de Tejeda, and centrepiece of the **Bentayga Archeology Park**. The road stops at a car park just short of the rock, from where it's easy to recognize the volcanic origins of many of the surrounding features. The **Centro de Interpretación** here (daily 10am–6pm; free) has displays on the geological story behind this landscape as well as on the cultural significance of the area and on episodes from the Spanish conquest of the Canaries, though the labelling is in Spanish only. The terrain around Bentayga, like that around Roque Nublo belongs to a phase of volcanic activity over three million years ago. Roque Bentayga was sacred to the Canarios and is the site of an *almogarén* (see p.186) like the one at Cuatro Puertas. The south side of the rock is riddled with cave dwellings, access to which – and to the rock in general – is restricted; call ☎928 381 368 (no English spoken; guided visits only) for information on visits. A little over 1km west of Roque Bentayga along a hair-raisingly narrow road (signposted La Solana) is **El Roque de Cuevas del Rey**, where an

artificial cave complex built by the Canarios in pre-conquest times includes grain silos and the Cueva del Guayre, one of the largest artificial caves on the island (same number as Bentayga for information on visiting). Bizarrely, a few inhabited houses huddle at the foot of the rock on this spectacular, but hardly cosy, ridge.

Tejeda

Pin-neat, basking in sunshine and brilliantly white against the green landscape, the large village of Tejeda adds an improbably domestic scale to the Cumbre's grandiose landscape, sitting 1000m above sea level below the lip of the Caldera de Tejeda. In the spring the area is a mass of flowering almond trees and in early February Tejeda celebrates the fiesta of the Almendro en Flor (Almond Festival; see p.177). The village is known for its almond biscuits and for its *bienmesabe*, the almond and honey confection found on dessert menus throughout the island. You can buy both from the Dulcería Nublo on the main street. Tejeda is remote from the main population centres of the island but it's not uncultured: the **Museo de Esculturas**

▲ ROQUE BENTAYGA

▲ TEJEDA

de Abraham Cárdenes (C/ Leocadio Cabrera ☎928 666 189; Tues–Fri 11am–3.30pm, Sat 11.30am–2.30pm, Sun 11.20am–4pm, closed first two weeks in Aug; free) contains works by the Tejeda-born sculptor Abraham Cárdenes and also attracts touring exhibitions. The church of Nuestra Señora del Socorro nearby is an odd structure with almost pagoda-like tiled roofs; it was built to replace a predecessor destroyed by fire in 1920.

Cruz de Tejeda and Pozo de las Nieves

A scant couple of kilometres to the northeast of Tejeda but many hundreds of metres higher, the crossroads of Cruz de Tejeda is where the principal roads of the interior cross. It also marks the point where the trade winds hit the top of the island, and so marks a noticeable change in climate zones from sunny Tejeda to the cooler, cloudier and wetter conditions that prevail around Vega de San Mateo. During the day the roadside here is lined with market stalls selling handicrafts, rum and local delicacies to the coach parties that pause for lunch in one of the busy restaurants. This is also the site of the island's parador, closed for many years but scheduled to re-open as a luxury hotel at the end of 2006 (🖳 www.parador.es). A few steps to the south of the tourist hubbub and the parador is one of the more extraordinary of the island's views, over Tejeda to Roque Bentayga, its outline the largest of a series of blue shapes shimmering in the haze. To the east, along the **Ruta Centro de las Cumbres**, a *mirador* shares the view, and also contains a visitor centre, the Centro de Interpretación Degollada Becerra, closed for rebuilding as this book went to press. About 4km beyond the *mirador* a side turning leads to a car park at **Pozo de Las Nieves**, the "snow well" where snow was once collected for use at the Hospital de St Martín in Las Palmas or for the manufacture of ice cream. The peak just above the car park is the highest point on the island at 1949m; when it does snow up here – as it did in the winter of 2004–5 – it makes the TV news and locals jump into their cars to see the phenomenon for themselves. What most visitors come to Pozo de las Nieves to see, however, is the extraordinary view across the centre of the island to Roque Nublo and, on the horizon, the peak of Mount Teide on Tenerife. It's particularly beautiful at sunset when the clouds pouring over the lip of the Caldera de Tejeda break like waves against the base of Roque Nublo; note that it can get bitterly cold up here after the sun goes down. The road ends at the car park, so you have to return to the main GC-130.

Caldera de los Marteles

East of Pozo de las Nieves the road descends through lush pine forests, the roadway often carpeted with rust-red pine needles, to the Caldera de los Marteles. This beautiful volcanic crater is a much gentler landscape feature than most, its eroded sides thick with vegetation and its shallow floor given over to agriculture. From the GC-130 road a footpath leads the 4km or so down into the upper reaches of the Barranco de Guayadeque.

Montañon Negro and the Caldera Pinos de Gáldar

Northwest from Cruz de Tejeda the high GC-150 road follows the rim of Tejeda's caldera, passing recently fire-damaged forest and the suitably menacing (though now dormant) cinder black cone of Montañon Negro, the most recent volcano to erupt on Gran Canaria, some 3000 years ago. Though the cone's flanks are softened a little by pine forest, the bare, smooth black ash still looks remarkably fresh. The road rejoins the GC-21 at the Caldera Pinos de Gáldar, a dramatic volcanic crater created at the same time as the Montañon Negro. The trade winds hit this corner of the island with such force that it's sometimes difficult to stand at the *mirador* overlooking the crater – it's perfectly safe, but can be quite literally breathtaking. If you brave the winds, the reward is a panoramic view of the north of the island.

▲ CRUZ DE TEJEDA MARKET

▲ ARTENARA

Artenara

A statue of Christ watches over Artenara, the highest village on Gran Canaria at 1270m and focus of the least-populated municipality on the island, with fewer than 2000 inhabitants. Always an isolated place, its isolation increased early in 2005 when landslides triggered by the worst winter storms in thirty years blocked the road to Tejeda – though it had reopened by the end of that year. Many of the dwellings here, even those with conventional housefronts, lie underground, burrowed deep into the soft volcanic rock and, though the centre of the village is dominated by the nineteenth-century church of San Mateo, it's for just such a subterranean construction, the **Ermita de la Virgen de la Cuevita** chapel and the effigy of the Virgin it contains, that the village is best known. Each year in August the image of the Virgin is taken in procession from the chapel to San Mateo church to celebrate the village's main

feast days and then, on the last Sunday of August is returned to her cave; a firework display completes the festivities. The chapel is a few minutes' walk uphill from the centre of the village – it's well signposted – but once you get there it's frankly rather damp and claustrophobic inside, though the lovely views on the way make the walk worthwhile. Back in the village centre, the building on Avenida Alcalde Manuel Lujan Sanchez that houses the tourist office also houses the **Centro de Recuperación de Artesanía** (Mon–Fri 9.15am–3pm, Sat 10.15am–2.30pm; ☎928 666 102; free) which extends back into the side of the hill, its rooms used for temporary exhibitions on subjects of local ethnographic or historic interest and to display locally made pottery.

Pinar de Tamadaba

One of the key constituents of the World Biosphere Reserve, the Pinar de Tamadaba is a high-altitude pine forest covering the upper slopes of the 1444-metre peak of Tamadaba. After the car park at Cortijo de la Tirma – from which some of the forest's longer paths fan out – the road becomes a one-way, circular drive, offering access to various woodland paths and giving stunning views down to the coast and across to Tenerife. A signposted path descends from the roadside to Lugarejos and El Hornillo and from there down into the Barranco de Agaete. Just after the campsite turnoff a path climbs up to the Tamadaba peak itself. It's a fairly easy 25-minute walk uphill through the forest, the air pure enough to allow great beards of lichen to hang down from the branches. All the way up there are tantalizing glimpses of Tenerife. To get the very best views at the top you need to scramble the last few metres onto the peak; from here, you can see Tenerife to the west and Roque Bentayga and the landscapes of the island's interior to the east.

Vega de Acusa

The placid, flat tableland of Vega de Acusa is perched high above the deep *barrancos* that run down towards the coast at La Aldea. Reached via a turning off the Tamadaba road, it looks like a location from a spaghetti western, its pastoral landscape and solitary whitewashed chapel contrasting with the drama of the surrounding mountains, and its flanks dotted with cave dwellings. The few roads on the plateau are narrow and rough, and if you've come by car it's best to park by the church and explore these tracks on foot – one follows the edge of the

plateau, from where the views towards Roque Bentayga are spectacular. On the north side of the plateau, to the right of the church, a stunning but narrow and twisting minor road descends past a windmill and a series of reservoirs to San Nicolás de Tolentino.

Hotels

El Refugio

Cruz de Tejeda ☎928 666 513, ⊛www.hotelelrefugio.com. In a magnificently scenic setting right on the lip of the Caldera de Tejeda at Cruz de Tejeda, this small country hotel has just ten rooms, a pool and sunny garden for sunbathing. Rooms are air-conditioned, with artisan-made furniture and en-suite bath, plus TV and phone. There's a sauna, a private *mirador* giving access to one of the finest views on the island, and they have mountain bikes for guest use. The hotel also has a large and popular restaurant. €64.

▲ PINAR DE TAMADABA

Las Tirajanas

C/Oficial Mayor José Rubio, San Bartolomé de Tirajana ☎928 123 000, ⊛www.hotel-lastirajanas. com. Strikingly sited on a bluff overlooking the town of San Bartolomé de Tirajana and 1000m above sea level, *Las Tirajanas* is a smart mountain resort hotel with relaxed, spacious public areas including a restaurant. Rooms are tastefully decorated in a modern Canarian style, with wooden furniture, terracotta tiles and (in the junior suites) four poster beds. All 52 rooms have a balcony and share the hotel's panoramic views. There's a pool and a spa. €80.

Cafés and restaurants

La Candelilla

Carretera de Ayacata ☎928 172 281. Daily 8.30am–7pm. Something of a favourite with the bikers who tour the centre of the island at weekends, *La Candelilla*'s shady terrace is in an idyllic spot just outside the village of Ayacata, close to Roque Nublo. They serve good, inexpensive Canarian dishes such as marinated fried rabbit with *papas arrugadas* and *mojo picón*, and grilled fish. Service is friendly, if not particularly swift.

Restaurante Centenario

Hotel Rural El Refugio, Cruz de Tejeda ☎928 666 513. Daily 10am–8pm. The big, busy restaurant at the *El Refugio* is a popular pitstop in Cruz de Tejeda, with its own direct access from the main road separate from the hotel. Dishes include roast lamb marinated in dry Malvasia wine with herbs and onions, and the three-course lunch menu with wine or beer for €15 is good value.

Santiago El Grande

Hotel Las Tirajanas, C/Oficial Mayor José Rubio, San Bartolomé de Tirajana ☎928 123 000. Daily 1–4.30pm & 7–10.15pm. Diners at *Las Tirajanas* share the same breathtaking mountain panoramas as the hotel's guests. The cooking here is broadly Canarian, with *queso frito* (fried cheese) or prawns in garlic to start followed by hake in salsa verde, *morcilla* or sirloin steaks. Prices are reasonable, with main courses around €10–15, and the dining room is tastefully decorated and spacious. The hotel also has its own vineyard.

The Costa Canaria

At the southern tip of Gran Canaria, the wonderfully spacious golden sands pile up to form the shimmering dunes of Maspalomas, the most startling landscape in the south of the island and the centrepiece of the resort complex known as the Costa Canaria. Forty-five years ago this was a lonely stretch of coast backed by semi-arid farmland, neglected for most of its history and once the haunt of European and North African pirates. But in 1961 Count Alejandro del Castillo, the local landowner, organized a competition – won by a French company – to create a new resort. The result was something akin to a tourist gold rush, as hotels and apartment blocks, leafy bungalow complexes and stark concrete shopping centres engulfed the original village of Maspalomas (whose name means simply "more pigeons") and sun, sea, sand and pulsating nightlife have been provided with ruthless efficiency ever since. Over the years, the various districts have developed their own character; San Fernando is where the locals live, San Agustín is quiet and select, Playa del Inglés is the noisy haven of clubbers and gay visitors, and Maspalomas is low rise and laid back, with lush gardens, long avenues of palms and a golf course. Recent years have seen renewed development as huge resort hotels and shopping malls rise along the cliffs of Meloneras to the conurbation's west.

Gran Karting Club

Carretera General del Sur, km 46, Tarajalillo ☎928 157 190, ☻www.grankartingclub.com. Daily: April–Sept 11am–10pm; Oct–March 10am–9pm. €15 for 15 minutes, junior circuit €10, infants €7. Speed fiends will love the main track here – it's 1650m long, enabling karts to reach 80kph. There's a separate, shorter

---

Visiting the Costa Canaria

Within Playa del Inglés and Maspalomas, **buses** are chiefly of use for east-west travel, though many routes run north-south part way along Avenida de Tirajana, the principal avenue of Playa del Inglés. The urban area is very spread out, particularly in low-rise Maspalomas, so local buses are useful if you're travelling from one end of the conurbation to the other, but most visitors make use of the cheap taxis (☎928 766 767 or ☎928 142 634). The island government maintains a **tourist information office** (Mon–Fri 9am–9pm, Sat 9am–noon; ☻www.grancanaria.com) on Avenida de España at the entrance to the Yumbo Centre; the town council runs an office at the Mirador Campo de Golf in Maspalomas (Mon–Fri 9am–3.30pm) and another at the Centro Anexo II on the beach in Playa del Inglés (Mon–Fri 9am–9pm, Sat 9am–1pm).

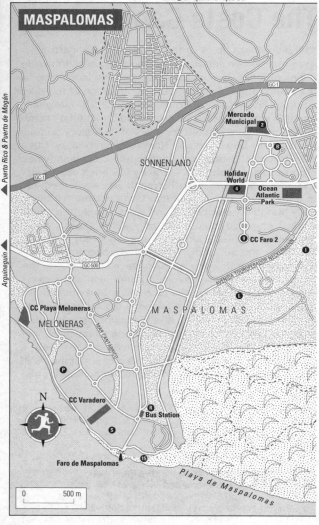

course for 12–16 year olds and a miniature version for younger children. Wear flat shoes and nothing too loose.

Real Aeroclub de Gran Canaria

Carretera General del Sur, km 46.5, Tarajalillo ☎928 762 447. This small aerodrome, wedged between the sea and the coast road, is home

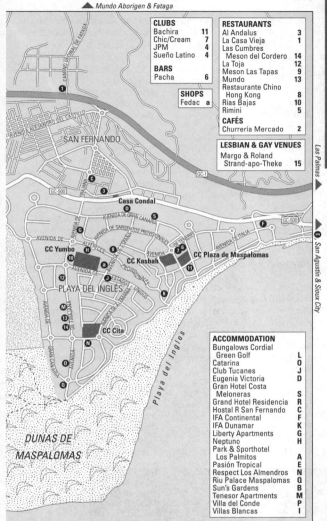

CLUBS
Bachira	11
Chic/Cream	7
JPM	4
Sueño Latino	4

BARS
Pacha	6

SHOPS
Fedac	a

RESTAURANTS
Al Andalus	3
La Casa Vieja	1
Las Cumbres Meson del Cordero	14
La Toja	12
Meson Las Tapas	9
Mundo	13
Restaurante Chino Hong Kong	8
Rias Bajas	10
Rimini	5

CAFÉS
Churrería Mercado	2

LESBIAN & GAY VENUES
Margo & Roland Strand-apo-Theke	15

ACCOMMODATION
Bungalows Cordial Green Golf	L
Catarina	O
Club Tucanes	J
Eugenia Victoria	D
Gran Hotel Costa Meloneras	S
Grand Hotel Residencia	R
Hostal R San Fernando	C
IFA Continental	F
IFA Dunamar	K
Liberty Apartments	G
Neptuno	H
Park & Sporthotel Los Palmitos	A
Pasión Tropical	E
Respect Los Almendros	N
Riu Palace Maspalomas	Q
Sun's Gardens	B
Tenesor Apartments	M
Villa del Conde	P
Villas Blancas	I

to a couple of outfits offering parachute jumps over the dunes of Maspalomas. Skydive Gran Canaria (☎928 157 325, ⓦwww.skydivegrancanaria.es; tandem jump from €155) offers tandem and night-time jumps and courses; rival Jump for Life (☎928 157 000, ⓦwww.jump-for-life.com; €199 per tandem jump) is a similar operation; they can both arrange to collect you from your accommodation in a minibus. The airstrip is also the departure point for helicopter sightseeing tours of the island (ⓦwww.bluecanarias.com; from €50 for a 10-minute flight).

Bahía Feliz

Bahía Feliz has some of the best-designed holiday apartments on the island and a purpose-built village plaza with an adequate selection of restaurants and bars. It is, however, extremely quiet and relatively remote from its more animated neighbours and thus appeals to a less raucous clientele.

Playa del Águila

Playa del Águila is smaller and even more low-key than Bahía Feliz, and has a pebbly beach that is not terribly attractive. For active visitors, however, there is some appeal as the home of the Dunkerbeck Windsurfing School (ⓉT649 538 333, ⓦwww.dunkerbeck-windsurfing.com), owned and operated by world windsurfing champion Björn Dunkerbeck. For more information, see p.177.

Sioux City

Cañon del Águila ⓉT928 762 573. Bus #29 from Maspalomas and Playa del Inglés. 10am–5pm. €14, children €7. A successful recreation of a Wild West frontier town, Sioux City was originally built in 1975 as a set for the Lee Van Cleef spaghetti western *Take a Hard Ride*. Today it's a big hit with dads and children in particular, and the location, in a deep, rugged *barranco*, is suitably wild and western-looking. Wandering through the town you'll encounter actors in costume playing out their roles – the sheriff cleaning his gun, or a cowboy training his horse – plus there's a saloon, church and jail to have a look round, and you can buy wanted posters or cowboy gear as souvenirs. To see Sioux City at its most animated, however, catch one of the frequent shows, during which you might see stunt riding, saloon girls dancing or Mexican bandits shooting up the town.

San Agustín

San Agustín was one of the first and most upmarket resorts to be developed in the south of the island and it retains a somewhat quiet, relaxed atmosphere. The two sandy beaches – the broad, darkish Playa San Agustín itself and the similar Playa de las Burras to the west – are linked by an attractive, traffic-free clifftop walk; a few fishing boats still pull up on the Playa de las Burras and the apartment complexes here are small and well-established. The air of refinement is

▲ SIOUX CITY

▲ SAN AGUSTÍN

most evident in the **Casino Gran Canaria** (*Meliá Tamarindos Hotel,* C/Las Retamas 3; daily 8pm–4am; free) where smart dress amd your passport will give you access to American roulette, blackjack, poker and the usual slot machines.

Playa del Inglés

Big, brash Playa del Inglés is the archetypal Spanish package tour resort, a place where German oompah bars jostle British pubs, Chinese restaurants stand next to Irish bars and the restaurant of choice is the ubiquitous steak house. It's also unmistakably the liveliest resort in the south of the island, with accommodation to suit all tastes and budgets, excellent nightlife for heterosexual and gay visitors alike – centred on the Kasbah and Yumbo shopping centres respectively – and annual Carnival celebrations second on the island only to those of Las Palmas. Much of the accommodation has been refurbished in recent years, and some of the unashamedly modern architecture is beginning to look fashionable in a retro way – a good example is the Sol Barbacán apartment

complex on Avenida Tirajana, its outlandish curves vaguely resembling a sports stadium. And amid all the concrete there is plenty of lush, mature subtropical foliage, so that these days it's really only the vibrant but run-down *centros comerciales* that offend the eye. The resort is roughly triangular, coming to a point in the south, where the busy Avenida de Tirajana terminates just short of a

▲ SOL BARBACÁN

PLACES

The Costa Canaria

spectacular *mirador* overlooking the Maspalomas dunes at the end of Avenida de Tirajana. A pleasant clifftop walk leads east from the *Riu Palace Hotel* to the Avenida de Alfereces Provisionales, which snakes down an urban *barranco* to provide the easiest access to the vast, sandy beach, too big ever to be truly overcrowded. It's patrolled, well provided with sun loungers and has snack kiosks every few hundred metres. The beach narrows as it reaches the headland of Punta de Maspalomas, where the dunes finally reach the sea and mark the transition to neighbouring Maspalomas beach.

The dunes of Maspalomas

Created by a unique combination of sea and wind (and not blown in from Africa as previously thought) the dunes of Maspalomas are a stunning sight and deservedly on every visitor's itinerary. The beauty and richness of the flora and birdlife that colonize the western, stable portion of the dunes create an ecosystem unique in the Canary Islands and mean that more than 400 hectares of

the dunes and adjacent *charca* (lagoon) are a protected nature reserve, the ideal conditions encouraging large numbers of migratory birds to rest here on their seasonal journeys between Europe and Africa. To the east, the bare, shifting portion of the dunes retains a pristine, desert-like appearance. **Access** is restricted to either the path that leads from the *mirador* at the *Hotel Riu Palace* in Playa del Inglés (where there's a small **information office**; Mon–Fri 9.30am–12.30pm & 4.30–7pm), or from along the shore from Playa del Inglés or the Faro de Maspalomas.

From the heart of the dunes, the views of the island's mountainous interior are superb and the bustle of the surrounding conurbation seems very distant, with only the *Riu Palace* and Maspalomas lighthouse as significant landmarks. Secluded areas of the dunes are popular with naturists and are a famous, if fairly discreet, gay cruising ground, so be prepared to see the odd bit of naked flesh along with the wildlife. You might also encounter a camel train

▲ THE DUNES OF MASPALOMAS

▲ MASPALOMAS BEACH

PLACES The Costa Canaria

laden with a cargo of nervous holidaymakers – if you want to join them, head along the western shore of the lagoon to Camello Safari Duna Oasis (daily 9am–4.30pm; ☎928 760 781).

Maspalomas

Long before the hotels, shopping centres and nightclubs there was a single architectural landmark in the very south of the island – the 51-metre **Faro de Maspalomas** lighthouse, built in the late nineteenth century to aid steamships travelling between Africa, Australia and America. Its solitude disappeared forever with the tourist boom in the 1960s and 1970s when the dense oasis of date palms behind it became the focus for a particularly upmarket strain of development, and today the numerous five-star hotels here help Maspalomas retain an aura of prestige. To the north and east, the golf course and villas give way to the low-rise district of **Campo Internacional**, centred on the Faro 2 shopping

complex and consisting largely of bungalows with lush gardens and swimming pools though also holding two major leisure attractions. The first, **Holiday World** (☎928 730 498, ®www.holidayworld-maspalomas.com), is a multi-purpose entertainment complex with an indoor leisure centre fronting a traditional funfair (Mon–Thurs 6–11pm, Fri & Sat 6pm–1am, free entry, buy points for rides at the entrance) with big wheel, roller coaster and carousels. It also has a bowling alley (Sun–Thurs 10am–2am, Fri & Sat 10am–5am), pool tables, bars and restaurants, two discos and an impressive gym and spa, complete with rooftop pool and lido. A few hundred metres to the east of Holiday World is **Ocean Atlantic Park** (June–Sept Mon–Fri 10am–6pm, Sat & Sun 10am–7pm; Oct–May daily 10am–5pm; €19, children €13; ☎928 764 361, ®www.oceanatlanticpark.com), the most central of Maspalomas' two water parks. Water slides and spirals of varying degrees of severity are the attraction at this one, though there's also mini golf. For those who prefer seawater to swimming pools, **Maspalomas beach** is every bit as splendid as that at Playa del Inglés, with similar facilities including a Red Cross post, sun loungers to hire and snack bars. There are specific naturist and gay sections, the former well marked and the latter clustered around snack bar no.7. Be aware that the sea gets discernibly rougher towards the Punta de Maspalomas headland.

Aqualand Aqua Sur

Carretera Palmitos Park, km 3 ⓦwww. aqualand.es. Buses #45 or #70 from Maspalomas. Daily: April–Oct 10am– 6pm; Nov–March 10am–5pm. €21, children 3–12 €15. Billing itself as the largest water park in the south of the island, Aqualand has all the slides – no fewer than 33 of them – pools and sunbathing terraces you could possibly

▲ PALMITOS PARK

need. The latest attraction is the fearsome Tornado slide with sound and light effects. Given the rather steep entry charge it's worth making a day of it. There's a variety of places to eat, from snacks and ice creams to burgers and a restaurant, and if the water palls you can always shop for pearls at Perla Canaria next door.

Banana Park

Carretera Palmitos Park, km 4 ☎928 141 475, ⓦwww.bananapark-maspalomas.com. Bus #45 or #70 from Maspalomas. Daily 10am–5pm. €7, children free; Banana Park is a working organic banana and pawpaw plantation and citrus grove where in addition to visiting a traditional fruit plantation visitors can learn about aloe vera, sugar cane, strelitzias, mangoes and tomatoes before sampling the fresh juices of the fruits. There's also a free-flight canary aviary, a butterfly house, farm animals including donkeys and camels, and a souvenir shop selling traditional island produce including *mojo* sauces, wines and liqueurs. It may not be as ambitious in its scope as some of the other parks, but Banana Park is at least derived from the traditional agriculture of the island and that makes it worth a visit.

Palmitos Park

Barranco de los Palmitos ☎928 140 276, ⓦwww.palmitospark.es. Buses #45 or #70 from Maspalomas. Daily 10am–6pm. €17, children €12. Palmitos Park is an excellent combination of zoo, aviary and botanical garden in a beautiful mountain valley a few kilometres north of Maspalomas. It's known particularly for its parrots, but there are also flamingoes, cockatoos, hornbills, toucans, a children's farm and some languid caiman crocodiles from South America. Highlights include the free-flight aviary, a wonderful tropical aquarium, the butterfly and orchid houses and the lovely terraced cactus garden. Regular daily shows with performing parrots are a hit with children.

Meloneras

The low cliffs to the west of the Faro de Maspalomas have witnessed an extraordinary burst of new development in recent years. Vast four- and five-star resort hotels and wide tracts of smart suburban housing have spread along a previously barren stretch of coast towards the little marina development of Pasito Blanco. From the Faro, a popular but still incomplete clifftop promenade leads past this parade of hotels and shopping arcades towards the rather stoney little beach of Meloneras. In an attempt to reduce the coast's dependency on low-priced package holidays, the **Maspalomas Congress Centre**, an elegant and impressive venue a few hundred metres inland from the hotel strip, opened in 2000 but, embarrassingly, was forced to close during the winter of 2004–5 to rectify a series of construction and design defects. It was scheduled to reopen again in November 2006, when it will once again provide a venue not just for the lucrative conference and exhibition trade but for classical and pop concerts and various events, including Maspalomas' gay pride.

Pasito Blanco

Bus #32 from Maspalomas. For now, the sleepy little yacht harbour of Pasito Blanco sits in quiet isolation west of Meloneras, though development is slowly encroaching. Vehicle access to the marina and its residential development is tightly controlled, but you can park outside and stroll in for a look if you're curious. Two kilometres to the north of the harbour, the European Space Agency's Maspalomas Ground Station (INTA Estacion Espacial de Maspalomas) – which played a key role in tracking the Apollo launches of the 1970s – stands on high ground at Montaña Blanca.

San Fernando

The lively *barrio* of San Fernando lies to the north of Playa del Inglés and Maspalomas across the GC-500 highway and contains the remnants of the original village of Maspalomas. By far the most Canarian district in the Costa Canaria conurbation – it was largely built in the early 1960s to house farmers dispossessed by the construction of the resort on their land – it has all the facilities of a real town, including a football stadium, municipal market, town square and lively shopping centre. It's also where some of the more authentic restaurants of the conurbation are to be found. Along Avenida Marcial Franco are some pre-development buildings, namely the little chapel of **San Fernando el Chico** (key from church of San Fernando on Avda Tejeda) and the **Casa Condal** (Mon–Fri 10am–8pm; free), an imposing farmhouse that now houses art exhibitions by local artists as well as a fascinating display on the history of the area, including startling photos of the coast before tourism arrived.

▲ CASA CONDAL, SAN FERNANDO

Mundo Aborigen

Carretera Playa del Inglés-Fataga,
km 6 ☎928 172 295. Bus #18 from
Maspalomas and San Fernando. Daily
9am–6pm. €12, children free. Spread
over a sunny mountainside
above San Fernando, Mundo
Aborigen is an admirable
attempt to re-create the lifestyle
and landscapes of pre-Hispanic
Gran Canaria and its inhabitants.
The indigenous vegetation,
reconstructed round stone
houses and clear labelling of
exhibits give an informative
introduction to the island's past.
Topics covered include the
social hierarchies, belief systems,
burial rituals and craft skills of
the first Canarios – generally
depicted as tall and fair – who
came to the island from North
Africa around 2–3000 years
ago. They lacked metal tools
but nevertheless worked wood
and stone with skill to create
their homes. Highlights include
the house of a *guanarteme* or
nobleman and
the *tagoror*
or council
chamber, both
of which
are brightly
decorated, in
contrast to the
stark simplicity
of the homes
of the poor.

Mirador de Fataga

Carretera Playa
del Inglés-Fataga.
The Mirador
de Fataga
is a popular
viewing spot

▲ MIRADOR DE FATAGA

for bus tours and a frequent stopping off point for super-fit cyclists on the twisting, narrow but well-surfaced road to Fataga. The *mirador* gives splendid views down to the coast and into the deep, rocky Barranco de Fataga, and also marks the point at which the road begins its spectacular journey into the island's interior.

Hotels

Catarina
Avda Tirajana 1, Playa del Inglés ☏928 762 812, ⊛www.lopesanhr. com. Nicely refurbished 1960s hotel on the quieter, southern stretch of Avenida de Tirajana. There's a stark, rather elegant minimalist foyer, while the rooms are spacious and tasteful, and those on the higher floors have good views of the dunes and mountains. Facilities include a Tahitian-style pool and lido complex. €130.

Eugenia Victoria
Avda de Gran Canaria 26, Playa del Inglés ☏928 762 500, ⊛www. bullhotels.com. Vast, comfortable hotel that pitches itself at a younger clientele. Public areas are nothing special, but rooms are attractive enough, pricing is fairly keen, there's a free shuttle bus to the beach and its sporting facilities, including tennis and squash courts, a well-equipped gym and sauna are popular and open to non-residents. €80.

Grand Hotel Residencia
Avda del Oasis 32, Maspalomas ☏928 723 100, ⊛www.grand-hotel-residencia.com. Relatively small, secluded five-star boutique hotel, built in the form of two-storey villas and set in the luxuriantly subtropical surroundings of the Maspalomas Oasis. The architecture and furnishings are traditionally Spanish/Moorish in style, and there's a restaurant serving international and Canario cuisine. It shares some facilities with its trendier, larger sister hotel, the *Palm Beach*. €408.

Gran Hotel Costa Meloneras
Costa Meloneras ☏928 128 144, ⊛www.lopesanhr.com. With its grandiose colonial-style architecture, spacious grounds and lofty public spaces, the clifftop *Costa Meloneras* was one of the first outsized seafront fantasy palaces of the new Meloneras district. It's a smart four-star resort hotel, complete with infinity pool, grotto-like spa and a number of bars and restaurants, while its 1136 rooms are tastefully furnished in modern style with warm colour schemes. €190.

PLACES The Costa Canaria

▲ GRAN HOTEL COSTA MELONERAS

IFA Continental

Avda de Italia 2, Playa del Inglés ☏928 760 033, ⊛www.ifacanarias.es. A big concrete hotel with a slightly institutional feel, the *Continental* might not win prizes for charm, but it's in a convenient location, offers very good rooms for the money and has a welcoming family atmosphere. €78 half board.

IFA Dunamar

C/Helsinki 8, Playa del Inglés ☏928/773 465, ⊛www.ifacanarias. es. If you're going to stay at the seaside you might as well have a sea view, and the staid but well-appointed *Dunamar* – which attracts a predominantly German clientele – fits the bill. Rooms are comfortable and spacious, if a little bland in decor, and the terraced outdoor areas are imaginatively done, but note that the streets behind can be noisy late at night. €194 half board.

Neptuno

Avda Alfereces Provisionales 29, Playa del Inglés ☏928 777 492, ⊛www.hotel-neptuno.com. The *Neptuno* is no beauty, but clever refurbishment of the public areas has produced an inspired, funky mix of original 1960s details and smart modernity. During Carnival and in summer it attracts a younger crowd, thanks to its close proximity to the Yumbo Centre. Rooms are en suite with blue and white ornamental azulejo tiles, TV and minibar; balconies have views of the pool and the less than restful Yumbo itself. €104.

Park & Sporthotel Los Palmitos

Barranco de los Palmitos 22 ☏928 142 100, ⊛www.lospalmitos. com. Small hotel in the idyllic surroundings of the Barranco de los Palmitos, overlooking Palmitos Park, complete with pool, tennis courts, pitch and putt, gym and practice nets for golf. And if that's not enough to tire you out, there are mountain bikes available and riding stables nearby. Rooms are modern and tastefully decorated. €204.

Riu Palace Maspalomas

Avda de Tirajana, Playa del Inglés ☏928 769 500, ⊛www.riu.com. The gleaming white, vaguely Moorish-style *Riu Palace* is a Costa Canaria landmark and the

▲ RIU PALACE HOTEL

only hotel in Playa del Inglés to possess an unobscured view of the sunsets across the dunes to the Maspalomas lighthouse. Most of its colonial-style rooms have sea views and there's a spacious, sunny lido with children's playground and pools. €254.

Villa del Conde

Mar Mediterráneo 7, Maspalomas ☎928 563 200, ⊛www.lopesanhr. com. From the outside, this new luxury hotel appears like a traditional Canario village, complete with "church" and "plaza"; inside, the spacious lobby incorporates bars, lounges and a giant crystal chandelier, while the rooms are spacious and stylish with hot colours and modern art. Depending on your taste, it's either highly kitsch or winningly audacious, but either way, it's certainly not bland. A thalassotherapy centre is planned and there are various restaurants and shops on site. €250.

Pension

Residencia San Fernando

C/La Palma 16, San Fernando ☎928 763 906. Clean but spartan *hostal*, with simply furnished twin-bedded rooms and shared facilities. Nothing fancy, but it's about the cheapest accommodation you'll get in the south. €18.50.

Self-catering

Bungalows Cordial Green Golf

Avda de Tjaereborg, Campo Internacional, Maspalomas ☎928 721 147, ⊛www.cordialcanarias. com. The "bungalows" in this large Andalucian-style complex are actually small, two-storey houses, including sixteen with two bedrooms that are ideal for families. Extensive, attractive pool areas, a minimarket on site and regular (if rather cheesy) entertainment add to the appeal as does its location close to bus stops and the Faro 2 shopping complex. You have to register online in order to book. €64.

Liberty Apartments

Avda de Tirajana, 32, Playa del Inglés ☎928 767 354, ⊛www.grupoliberty. com. Popular, centrally located one-bedroom apartments on the northern stretch of Avenida de Tirajana, convenient for banks, restaurants, shops and nightlife, but a little distant from the beach. The apartments sleep up to three people. If you can, try to get one with a balcony facing the spacious pool area at the back, as the street out front is one of the busiest in Playa del Inglés. €51.

Sun's Gardens

C/Virgo, Campo Internacional, Maspalomas ☎928 765 235, ⊛www.servatur.com. Situated in a quiet corner of the Campo Internacional, *Sun's Gardens* is the archetypal Maspalomas bungalow complex, attractively grouped around a pool, with subtropical plants and a basic bar/restaurant on site. It's a smaller complex than most and the accommodation is in simply furnished one-bedroom duplexes that sleep three (a fourth bed can be provided for €3 per night). Very good value for money, though note that they only accept cash payments. €40.

Tenesor Apartments

Avda de Tirajana 9, Playa del Inglés ☎928 764 831, ⊛TENESOR_ 9@hotmail.com Spacious,

Lesbian and gay accommodation

Gay and lesbian visitors attracted to the Costa Canaria by the extensive nightlife and the easygoing, gay-friendly attitude, have plenty of options for resting their heads after a heavy night.

Club Tucanes Avda de EE.UU 29, Playa del Inglés ☎928 760 558, ⌨www.clubtucanes.com. Just across the road from the Yumbo Centre, *Club Tucanes* is a very pleasant and central complex offering smart accommodation in stylish twins or double bungalows, each with satellite TV and CD player. The pool is clothing optional, and there's a complimentary buffet breakfast. €90.

Pasión Tropical C/Adelfas 6, San Agustín ☎928 770 131, ⌨www.pasion-tropical.com. Close to the beach in San Agustín, the small, intimate *Pasión Tropical* was one of the first exclusively gay complexes to break away from the budget format and offer a higher level of comfort and better facilities, including an open-air gym, whirlpool and sunbeds. Note it's a taxi-ride away from the Yumbo Centre. Rates include buffet breakfast and there's a minimum stay of one week. €85.

Respect Los Almendros Avda de Francia 3, Playa del Inglés ☎+44 870 770 0169 (UK number), ⌨www.respect-holidays.co.uk. Attractive, exclusively lesbian and gay bungalow complex opposite the Centro Comercial Cita, with swimming pool, gym facilities, Jacuzzi and on-site bar and restaurant. Bungalows are air-conditioned, sleep up to three and are decorated to a good standard. There are no restrictions on nude sunbathing. Book by phone via the UK. €85.

Villas Blancas C/Tjaereborg, Maspalomas ☎928 769 445, ⌨www.villasblancas.com. The longest-established gay complex on the island, Villas Blancas is a cluster of recently-furbished, air conditioned bungalows around a pool, bistro and bar next to the tennis club in the leafy, relaxed Campo Internacional district. Facilities include internet access, telephones and CD players in bungalows. There's a smaller, quieter offshoot – Club Villas Blancas – nearby. Gay men only. €75.

refurbished apartments close to the Yumbo, popular with gay and heterosexual travellers alike. The exterior is somewhat grim and prison-like but for a reason, since the lack of large windows on the street cuts down the noise a bit. Inside, the two-bedroom apartments are comfortable, there's a pool, and the location is excellent, with plenty of shopping and dining opportunities on the doorstep. €47.

Shops

Centro Comercial Cita

Avda de Francia ⌨www.cc-cita.com. The Cita Centre is a startling structure, its exterior decorated with vast mockups of famous world landmarks. Inside, the retail outlets focus on jewellery, cameras, and electrical and leather goods, and there's an open plaza with several restaurants, many of which are aimed primarily at German visitors. The seedy basement contains some of Playa del Inglés' more adult-oriented nightlife.

Centro Comercial Faro 2

Plaza Touroperador Holland International, Campo Internacional de Maspalomas ⌨www.faro2.es. The strikingly modern spiral layout and chic designer fashion stores give the Faro 2 an upmarket edge, and its relatively modest size and pleasant setting amid palms and gardens make it by far the most attractive *centro* comercial on the south coast, despite competition from newer complexes in nearby Meloneras. There's also a useful supermarket and a reasonable selection of restaurants.

Centro Comercial Yumbo

Avda de EE.UU 54 ⓦwww.cc-yumbo. com. The Yumbo is the largest *centro comercial* in Playa del Inglés, good for practical things like banks, currency exchange and pharmacies and with a few smart fashion and sportswear stores scattered among the cheap tourist tat. At night it transforms itself into the centre of the island's gay scene and is where the drag cabaret bars are found. It also functions as the town square for the conurbation and is a focus for both Gay Pride and the annual carnival celebrations.

Fedac

Centro Insular de Turismo, Avda de España, Playa del Inglés ☎928 772 445. Mon–Fri 10am–2pm & 4–7.30pm If you want to shop for more than beach things or a cheap leather jacket the government-run Fedac handicrafts store is the place to come. Located in the tourist office at the Yumbo Centre, it sells high quality, traditional and modern ceramics, textiles, jewellery, toys and gifts, all made in the islands.

Mercado Municipal

Avda de Alejandro del Castillo, San Fernando. Daily 8am–2pm; open air market Wed & Sat. The municipal market is a good stop for excellent fresh bread, vegetables and delicatessen items. It's busiest on Wednesdays and Saturdays when the stalls spread into the open area at the back of the market hall.

Cafés

Café Wien

CC Cita ☎928 760 380, ⓦwww.cafe-wien.org. Mon–Fri 9am–11pm, Sat & Sun 2–11pm. For some years the wonderful German-run *Café Wien* has served the best coffee and cakes in the south of the island – the rhubarb cream torte is especially delicious. Note that, for some reason, there's a strict demarcation to the tables: elderly German couples at the back, gay men on the terrace and everyone else in between.

Churrería Mercado

Mercado Municipal, Avda de Alejandro del Castillo, San Fernando ☎928 786 590. If you want to try the traditional Spanish breakfast of *chocolate con churros* (hot chocolate with doughnut-like strips to dip in) head out to this unpretentious little café in the municipal market on Wednesdays and Saturdays. It's open from 5.30am, so you could even take a cab there direct from the disco.

▲ CAFÉ WIEN

Restaurants

Al Andalus

C/Marcial Franco, Bloque 5, San Fernando ☎928 760 465. Daily noon–midnight. Excellent Andalucian-style tapas bar with an authentic atmosphere and largely local clientele. Three dishes – around €3 each – make a meal, and portions are big so you won't leave hungry. Try the meltingly sweet peppers with *melva* – a relative of the tuna – or fried *choco* (squid).

Hong Kong

Avda de España 12, Playa del Inglés ☎928 760 702. Daily noon–midnight. Large, showily decorated Chinese restaurant in basement premises close to the Yumbo Centre. The menu is mostly Cantonese and the food is reliable and inexpensive at €7 for a main course. The mirrored ceiling and red panelled walls create a glittering effect.

La Casa Vieja

El Lomo 139, Carretera de Fataga, San Fernando ☎928 762 736. Mon–Fri & Sun 1pm–midnight, Sat 1pm–12.30am. Stuck a little way out from San Fernando on the road to Fataga, *La Casa Vieja* is probably the most extrovert of the south coast's Canarian restaurants: the *parillada* of assorted meats (€19.50 for two) is flame-cooked on a vast open grill, the bread and *alioli* – a pungent garlic mayonnaise – are excellent, and there's frequently live music from a traditional Canarian folk band.

Las Cumbres Mesón del Cordero

Edificio Taidia, Avda de Tirajana, Playa del Inglés ☎928 760 941. Daily except Tues 1–4pm & 7pm–midnight. The name means "house of lamb", and wonderfully tender oven-cooked lamb, served simply on the bone with sauté potatoes, is the speciality of this Spanish restaurant. The rustic interior is enlivened by whole hams dangling from the rafters and stuffed animals and cuddly toys of all shapes and sizes. Mains are around €12.

▲ LAS CUMBRES MESÓN DEL CORDERO

La Toja

Avda de Tirajana 17 ☎928
761 196. Daily 1–4pm
& 7pm–midnight, closed
in June. This long-
established, rather
formal and upmarket
Galician restaurant
has a good reputation.
They serve steaks and
an extensive list of hot
and cold tapas, but
the very best option
is to go for one of the
wonderful fish dishes
like the excellent
grilled turbot for
around €12.

Martel House

CC Yumbo Planta 2 local
232/04 ☎928 767 793.
Daily 11am–midnight.
Large, bustling
steak house on a spacious
balcony that has the edge on
its numerous rivals thanks to
efficient, courteous service, a
decent selection of Spanish
wines and hearty portions of
meat, plus Spanish and Canarian
specialities, for €7–11.

▲ MUNDO

Mesón Las Tapas

Centro Comercial Faro 2, Local 206,
Maspalomas ☎928 761 594. Daily
11am–11pm. In the upmarket but
rather anodyne surroundings of
the Faro 2 shopping complex
in Maspalomas, *Meson Las Tapas*
flies the flag for the Hispanic
way of eating. It's really more
a steak house than a tapas bar,
but many tapas favourites are
nevertheless here, including
delicious *pimientos de padrón*,
queso manchego and *jamón serrano*,
all priced around €3.50.

Mundo

Apartamentos Tenesor, Avda de
Tirajana, Playa del Inglés ☎928
761 063. Tues–Sun 7pm–1am.

Sophisticated modern fusion
cooking in slick, minimalist
premises makes *Mundo* a
standout among Playa's
restaurants. The wontons of
black pudding with apple and
pine nuts are delicious, the
prices are reasonable for the
very high quality on offer
– mains €15 – and it attracts
a mixed crowd of visitors and
locals. Highly recommended.

Rias Bajas

Edificio Playa del Sol, Avda de Tirajana,
Playa del Inglés ☎928 764 033. Daily
1–4pm & 7pm–midnight. A bit more
expensive and a bit more plush
than the Playa del Inglés average,
Rias Bajas specializes in fish and
seafood, with the likes of grilled
turbot, monkfish in a green herb
sauce or a *zarzuela* fish stew to
share. Mains from €22.

Rimini

Avda de Gran Canaria 28, Playa
del Inglés ☎928 764 187, ☻www.
ristorantesrimini.com. Daily

noon–midnight. Bustling Italian restaurant in a glassy extension to an apartment block close to the Gran Chaparral shopping centre. The menu is familiar, with the usual pizza, pasta and more elaborate meat-based dishes for €7 and up. Salads are generous, and you should save space for dessert, which is probably the high point – the pancakes with orange sauce and ice cream are especially good. There's a sister restaurant close to the bars of the Plaza Maspalomas.

Bars

Beckham Bar

Top floor, CC Kasbah, Playa del Inglés. Daily 8pm–4am. Hooded sweatshirts and jeans are the style at *Beckham*, a dress-down alternative to *Chinawhite*, with a mixed line-up of local and English DJs attracting a marginally younger crowd. Music tends towards R&B.

Chinawhite...Costa!

Top floor, CC Kasbah, Playa del Inglés. Daily 10pm–4am. Playa's beautiful people – including many locals – dress up to get down to R&B and hip-hop in this, probably the smartest of the DJ bars atop the Kasbah. The minimalist decor of white leatherette bar stools and glass-topped tables creates the required "smart" ambience and the atmosphere is excellent.

Garage

CC Kasbah Playa del Inglés. Sun–Thurs 8pm–4am, Fri & Sat 8pm–4.30am. This popular *discobar* in the bowels of the Kasbah centre is less trendy and more laid back than some of its neighbours, with the DJs playing mainstream pop and house to an international crowd. There's a small outdoor space too.

Hippodrome Disco Bar

Centro Comercial Plaza de Maspalomas, Playa del Inglés. Daily 8pm–4am. *Discobar* aimed at British holidaymakers at the bottom of the Plaza shopping centre, with plenty of pool tables out front, chart hits on the decks and Carlsberg to drink.

Pacha

Edificio Maritim, Playa del Inglés ☏928 769 201. Daily 8pm–4am. Smart, relaxed Madrid-style *terraza* DJ bar which pulls in an older (25–45) age group to gyrate to the latin-tinged dance pop or relax on the comfy sofas outside. There's no cover charge and the happy hour offers two-for-one drinks in the early evening.

▲ PACHA

Clubs

Bachira

Avda de Italia 27, Playa del Inglés. Thurs–Sat midnight–6.30am. €7, includes first two drinks. Smart, spacious basement club opposite the Plaza de Maspalomas shopping centre, with slideshows, go–gos and three bars. It attracts a mostly Canario crowd. Music is mainstream dance pop; it's busiest around 4am.

Chic/Cream

Plaza de Maspalomas, Playa del Inglés. €15, includes first drink. Big, impressive and rather expensive disco associated with Cream in the UK and attracting a trendy, twenty-something crowd. Industrial decor matches the banging hard house and techno, and there are four bars, regular guest DJ spots, go-go dancers and acres of space in which to dance. A shop in the foyer sells body jewellery.

JPM

Holidayworld, Avda Touroperador TUI, Campo Internacional, Maspalomas. Fri & Sat midnight–6am. JPM is a big (2000 capacity) house and dance music club in Maspalomas, with 20,000 watts of sound, regular themed nights including Mexican and Hawaiian parties, a VIP area, and guest DJs including some international big names.

Sueño Latino

Holidayworld, Avda Touroperador TUI, Campo Internacional, Maspalomas. Fri & Sat 11pm–6am Slick salsa, bachata and meringue club with a Cuban theme to the decor and a rather older crowd than the house and techno clubs.

Live music & shows

Casino Palace Gran Canaria

C/Las Retamas 3, San Agustín ☎928 762 724, ⊛www.casino-palace. net. Set dinner/show menus from €49.50 Glitzy supper club at the casino, offering an extravagantly choreographed, somewhat Vegas-style floorshow – albeit on a smaller scale – with lavish costumes, ice skating and magic tricks to distract your attention from the rich three- and four-course dinner menus, which feature the likes of lobster salad and medallions of sirloin steak with mushrooms. There's also an à la carte menu.

Garbo's Dinner Theatre

Bahía Feliz ☎928 157 060, ⊛www. nordotel.com. Dinner and show €45. Singing waiters, chorus lines and broadway medleys accompany dinner at *Garbo's*, in the plush setting of a former opera house that closed after its first performance and remained dark for the next 22 years. Garbo's has evidently broken the curse since it opened in 1997.

Ricky's Cabaret Bar

Planta Baja, CC Yumbo, Playa del Inglés. Show nightly around midnight. Free. An accessible slice of drag cabaret that attracts as many heterosexual as gay punters, *Ricky's* packs them in every night for a rather British, end-of-the-pier mix of music, sequins, audience humiliation and karaoke, with a Spanish dance troupe every Monday. Nearby *Café LaBelle* offers a similarly tried-and-tested blend of entertainment to a less packed house.

Lesbian & gay bars and clubs

The Costa Canaria's enduring popularity with lesbian and gay holidaymakers is reflected in its huge gay nightlife scene, which quite out-glitters the straight scene and is focused on – though by no means limited to – the Yumbo Centre. The lesbian presence is small in comparison with the huge commercial gay scene, but lesbians will be welcome in all except the more cruisy men's bars.

Centro Comercial Yumbo By day the Yumbo is the largest shopping centre in Playa del Inglés, but by night it's probably the largest single concentration of gay bars and clubs in Europe. Evenings kick off after 10.30pm on the lowest level (Planta Baja) in one of the relaxed *terraza* bars like *Nestor* or *Adonis*, or at one of the drag cabaret bars where the drinks tend to be more expensive. There's a split between Anglophone and Germanic gay nightlife early in the evening, with the better beer on offer in German bars such as *Na Und?* and *Spartacus*. Later, it's a choice between the quirky – local TS and TV colour at *The Terry Show* or show tunes on video at *Centre Stage* – the cruisy, in dark bars like *Construction* and *Cruise*, or the trendier, dance-oriented video bars on the fourth floor, where the action moves progressively from *Tubos* via *Mykonos* to the packed, intimate *Mantrix. Heaven*, on the third floor, is an offshoot of the famous London club and is the largest and most spectacular gay disco in the island, with slick modern decor, sexy go-go dancers, drag queens on podiums and big-name DJs from the international circuit. *XL*, on floor 2 below the taxi rank, is a traditional last port of call for dancing and drinking before heading to bed.

Detox/Retox Avda de Tirajana, Playa del Inglés. Tues–Sun 6.30pm–2am. ⓦwww.detoxretox.com. Stylish, laid-back bar with an amusing gimmick: alongside the usual beers, cocktails and shots they offer a range of healthier fruit smoothies and milkshakes. At last, the fashion crowd has somewhere in Playa del Inglés to go and not drink.

First Lady Edificio Taidia, Avda de Tirajana, Playa del Inglés. Daily 8pm–2.30am. The Costa Canaria's only lesbian bar and music club is run by a couple of German women and is popular with locals and visitors alike. Gay men are welcome as guests. There's a nightly happy hour between 8–9.30pm.

Margo & Roland Strand-apo-Theke Oasis, Local 35–36, Maspalomas. Mon–Sat 11am–8pm. Perfectly located for a sundowner on the surfers' favourite section of Maspalomas beach, *Strand-apo-theke* is probably the most relaxed and convivial gay bar on the island. It's packed every afternoon with a predominantly male, German crowd, who seem to know all the words to the cheesy *schlager* tunes that belt out of the sound system.

The southwest coast

Few places have been transformed as radically by tourism as the once-barren *barrancos* of Gran Canaria's rocky southwest. Where once a few fishermen eked out a living, purpose-built resorts now cater to the needs of sun-starved northern Europeans, golf courses paint the arid landscape green, and even the beaches are artificial. At Puerto Rico, apartments climb high up the *barranco* sides to create the impression of a giant stadium, while at Patalavaca, hotels are wedged dramatically between cliffs and the sea. The beaches are smaller than at Maspalomas, but the sea beckons in other ways: Arguineguín and Puerto de Mogán remain real, working fishing ports, Puerto de Mogán's marina is a textbook example of sensitive tourist development, and Puerto Rico's harbour is the departure point for all kinds of sea adventures, from game fishing to windjammers and power boats. Away from all this, the Barranco de Mogán is one of the most fruitful valleys in Gran Canaria, while the remote black sand beach of Veneguera and the reservoir of Soria inland offer escapes from the crowds. Best of all, this coast has the island's most reliable sunshine record.

▲ SALOBRE GOLF

Salobre

Set in a natural amphitheatre, sheltered from the trade winds

Visiting the southwest

The southwest resorts lie at the far end of the GC-1 motorway, which ends just beyond Puerto Rico: beyond this, road conditions deteriorate markedly and the coast road is twisting, narrow and busy. **Parking** is relatively easy in Puerto Rico, Amadores and Playa de Mogán, less so elsewhere due to the constricted sites of many resorts. Useful **local buses** include the frequent #32 between Puerto de Mogán and Playa del Inglés and the #84 that links Puerto de Mogán with Mogán. In Puerto Rico, the local Guaguas Mogán shuttle between the CC Europa and Amadores for a flat fare of €0.90. The main tourist office is by the bus station and central traffic intersection in Puerto Rico (Avda de Mogán €928 560 029, ⊛www.mogan.es, open Mon–Fri 9.30am–2.30pm & 5–7pm, Sat 9.30am–2.30pm); the main taxi rank is also close by (☎928 152 740).

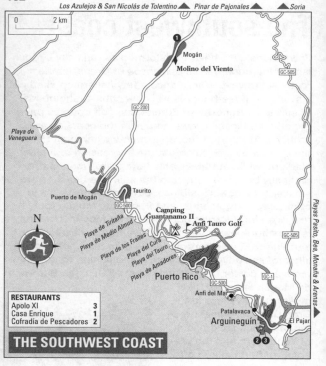

The southwest coast PLACES

Playas Pasito, Bea, Monaña & Arenas

0   2 km

❶ Mogán
Molino del Viento

GC-505

GC-200

Playa de Veneguera

Taurito
Puerto de Mogán
GC-500

N

Camping Guantanamo II
▶**Anfi Tauro Golf**

Playa de Tiritaña
Playa de Medio Almud
Playa de los Frailes
Playa del Cura
Playa del Tauro
Playa de Amadores

Puerto Rico

GC-505

GC-500   GC-1

Anfi del Mar

Patalavaca
Arguineguín   El Pajar
❷❸

RESTAURANTS	
Apolo XI	3
Casa Enrique	1
Cofradía de Pescadores	2

THE SOUTHWEST COAST

and with excellent views of the island's central mountains and the dunes at Maspalomas, the luxurious new 18-hole golf course and resort of Salobre is a world unto itself, screened from the motorway and approached from its own motorway exit. The golf course and its surrounding development is a surreal sight, the lush greens and opulent, stylishly modern private villas standing in stark contrast to the arid surroundings. A second course and a five-star Sheraton hotel were both scheduled to open in 2006. There's a restaurant with views over the greens and a shop on site.

Playa de Pasito Bea

Bus #32 from Maspalomas. Along the GC-500 old coast road are to be found some of the south's few remaining secluded beaches. The first of these, the **Playa de Pasito Bea**, is an attractively secluded sandy cove with wonderfully clear water. It's easy to reach, being just a couple of hundred metres down a dirt track from the coast road, but development is encroaching from the east and it may not preserve its isolated character much longer.

Playa de Montaña Arenas

Bus #32 from Maspalomas. West of the Playa de Pasito Bea the Playa de Carpinteras is not

Fiestas del Carmen

Each year in July, on successive Sundays closest to the saint's day on July 16 the two major fishing villages of the southwest, Arguineguín and Puerto De Mogán, celebrate the festival of Nuestra Señora del Carmen, the patron saint of sailors. On the first Sunday, an image of the Virgin heads a flotilla of fishing boats in procession from Arguineguín to Puerto de Mogán, where it "meets" that latter's Virgin, before the fleet sails home again, the boats festooned with balloons or decorations for the occasion. The following Sunday it's the turn of the fishermen of Puerto de Mogán to sail their fleet to Arguineguín and back in a mirror image of the previous week's festivities. The festival is also celebrated in Telde, San Nicolás de Tolentino and in the La Isleta district of Las Palmas.

especially appealing, a stoney stretch with a World War II pillbox. It does, however, have signposted parking off the GC–500 road and gives access on foot to the sandy nudist beach of Montaña Arenas, which is altogether more alluring. Access is along the Playa de Carpinteras and around the headland and is a bit of a scramble but well worth it – it's precisely this difficulty of access that has kept the beach unspoilt. Montaña Arenas gets its name from the vast mountain of sand behind that overlooks it. Note there are no facilities here.

El Pajar

Bus #32 from Maspalomas. Despite being overshadowed by the cement works on a nearby headland, El Pajar is a small, pleasant village with a gently shelving sandy beach and a few facilities, including an ice cream stall and a fish restaurant. East of here the coast is less developed with the rock and sand beach of **Llano de los Militares** and the pebbly **Playa de Triana** where you can camp provided you have a permit from the local authority of San Bartolomé de Tirajana (⊛www.maspalomas.com).

Arguineguín

Bus #32 from Maspalomas, Puerto Rico or Puerto de Mogán; regular ferries operated by Líneas Blue Bird or Líneas Salmón from Puerto Rico and Puerto de Mogán. Part resort, part fishing port, the pleasantly low-key little town of Arguineguín is no architectural wonder but, despite tourist development on its fringes, it retains the feel of a working port. There's a busy

PLACES The southwest coast

▼ BAY OF ARGUINEGUÍN

▲ SORIA

food market here every Tuesday morning (8am–2pm), and for sun-lovers there's a long curve of golden sand in the town itself and a shorter beach of sand and pebbles on the east side of town. To the west, an attractive coastal path winds around the rocky headland past small restaurants and a diving academy with English speaking instructors (see Essentials, p.175). It continues towards the tourist hotels to a tiny sand beach sheltered by a breakwater that creates, in effect, a natural saltwater pool for swimming. But it's Arguineguín's restaurants that are the real draw, particularly the fishermen's cooperative, the *Cofradía de Pescadores* (see p.142) which is inside the harbour gates.

Soria and the Pinar de Pajonales

Parched though the district of Mogán is at sea level, it becomes progressively greener as you head into the island's mountainous interior. One particularly beautiful journey is along the GC-505, which runs from the junction at El Pajar on the outskirts of Arguineguín to the reservoir at Soria, the largest on the island, with a dramatic high dam and a setting of green mountains. Pelargoniums tumble over the garden walls of the village of Soria overlooking the water and there are orange groves along the way.

From the hamlet of El Baranquillo Andrés, just before the reservoir, a rough and twisting road climbs higher still, taking you deep into the heart of the island to the pure air of the pine forest of Pinar de Pajonales, crossed by hiking trails. Freytag & Berndt's 1:75,000 Gran Canaria map marks the trails clearly.

Here, at the smaller reservoir of Cueva de las Niñas there's an inviting picnic site among the pine trees by the side of the lake, and a kiosk selling ice creams and snacks.

Patalavaca

The small, rather quiet resort of Patalavaca is in effect a westward extension of Arguineguín. Its tall hotels rather overshadow the small but pleasant sandy beach, which is reached via the car park in the *barranco*, entered from the landward side of the GC-500 coast road.

▲ PATALAVACA

There's a scattering of shops and restaurants along the coast road, but it's far more pleasant to dine in one of the restaurants along the traffic-free coastal path. This meanders from the attractive public lido (daily 10am–6pm; €6) past the luxury *Dunas Canarias* hotel towards the timeshare and marina complex of **Anfi del Mar**, whose public beach, the Playa de la Verga, is a dazzling strip of white, Caribbean-style sand.

Puerto Rico

Loved by some for its safe, family-friendly holiday environment and loathed by others for whom it represents the worst sort of overdevelopment, Puerto Rico is the largest resort in the southwest, a vast white amphitheatre scaling the slopes of an unusually wide *barranco*. The thousands of apartments are raked back against the hillsides in imitation of a sports stadium, so that each gets a balcony or patio and long hours of sunshine. The sea views get better the higher you go, and the apartment complexes at the very top are not overshadowed and consequently enjoy more

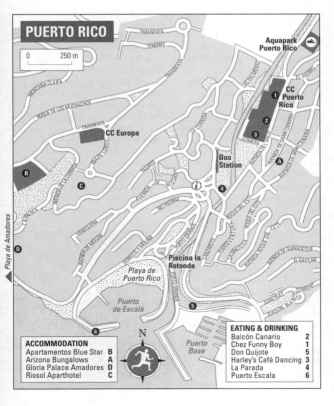

PUERTO RICO

0   250 m

Aquapark Puerto Rico

CC Puerto Rico

CC Europa

Bus Station

Playa de Amadores

Piscina la Rotonda

Playa de Puerto Rico

Puerto de Escala

Puerto Base

N

ACCOMMODATION
Apartamentos Blue Star   **B**
Arizona Bungalows   **A**
Gloria Palace Amadores   **D**
Riosol Aparthotel   **C**

EATING & DRINKING
Balcón Canario   2
Chez Funny Boy   1
Don Quijote   5
Harley's Café Dancing   3
La Parada   4
Puerto Escala   6

uninterrupted sun, so for those who don't mind being a bus or cab ride from the beach the higher, western parts of the town around the **Centro Comercial Europa** are a good bet. Larger complexes often have funicular railways connected with the road; without this or at least a lift, some of Puerto Rico's apartments are only for the fit, which perhaps explains their popularity among young, hard-partying singles.

The heart of the resort is defined by a series of subtropical gardens threading down the *barranco* from the grimly functional **Centro Comercial Puerto Rico** to the sea, offering a shady and mostly traffic-free approach to the man-made beach. The low-rise, small-scale complexes fringing the park represent the first phase of Puerto Rico's tourist development, predating the terraced hillsides. The **beach** is a pleasant, if not particularly large, curve of golden sand, backed by cafés and a public lido (Piscina La Rotonda; daily 10am–6pm; €6). To either side of the beach the leisure-oriented harbours are packed with yachts and with all manner of boats offering trips along the coast, including **Lineas Salmón** (Puerto Escala ☎649 919 383) and **Lineas Blue Bird** (Puerto Base ☎629 989 633), both of which use glass-bottomed boats to link Puerto Rico with Puerto de Mogán, Anfi and Arguineguín for around €9 return.

From the Puerto Escala, it's an easy one-kilometre stroll along a clifftop footpath to **Playa de Amadores**, the most recently constructed of Puerto Rico's man-made beaches. An 800-metre long crescent of fine sand, it's much

more spacious than the beach in Puerto Rico itself, and on a clear day it offers views across to Mount Teide on Tenerife. The resort area behind it is still developing, but there are already plenty of places to eat on the seafront. Just north of the Centro Comercial Puerto Rico is the **Aquapark Puerto Rico** (Avda Tomás Rocas Bosch ☎928 560 666; daily 10am–6pm; €20, child €14), whose attractions include slides, a giant waterfall and a children's pool. It's nicely landscaped, and you can buy snacks, drinks and simple meals.

Playa de Tauro and Playa del Cura

Playa de Tauro sits at the dry mouth of its eponymous *barranco*, a very humble little settlement strung out along a beach of pebbles and grey sand. There's a bar almost on the beach and a long-established campsite inland, but not much else – for the moment. The bulldozers are moving in here, and a short distance away in the Barranco del Lechugal there's a glitzy new nine-hole golf course, Anfi Tauro Golf, with attendant luxury villa developments that ape pre-Hispanic stone roundhouses. Plans for a shopping centre

▲ CLIFFTOP WALK, PUERTO RICO

▲ LAGO TAURITO OASIS

and a marina with space for 500 yachts have also been put forward. To the west of Playa de Tauro, the little *urbanizacíon* of Playa del Cura is pleasantly unimposing, like an isolated fragment of Puerto Rico, with a few apartment blocks hugging the hillsides and a short sandy beach backed by a promenade. It's relatively tasteful and there's a small *centro comercial,* but this is essentially a quiet beach resort.

Playa de Tiritaña

At the Barranco de Tiritaña, midway between Playa del Cura and Taurito, a steep, rough path leads down into the savagely narrow canyon to the sandy Playa de Tiritaña. Given the athleticism you'll need for the descent it's really only for the most enthusiastic nature lovers or determined nudists. Developers are closing in on the neighbouring *barrancos* of El Medio Almud and Los Frailes: the street lamps, palm trees and paved roads are in place, and it seems unlikely that their rock and sand beaches will remain the preserve of nudists much longer. Global buses travelling between

Puerto Rico and Puerto de Mogán pass along the coast road, but for the time being there are no stops and visitors to Tiritaña mostly arrive by car or by yacht.

Playa de Taurito

The Barranco de Taurito is one of the narrowest valleys yet developed as a resort, with mixed results. The big hotel and apartment complexes of Playa de Taurito are slick but monotonous to look at, so that you're more immediately conscious than in Puerto Rico that this is a purely artificial resort. The grey sandy beach is pleasant but rather small; the real focus of Playa de Taurito is the impressive **Lago Taurito Oasis** (Urbanizacíon Taurito ☎928 565 426; daily 10am–6pm; €9), an attractively landscaped lido with saltwater swimming pools, children's playgrounds, tennis and squash courts and a jogging circuit, all sheltering in a grove of date palms. There's also a diving school here. Continuing large scale development on the western flank of the barranco means some construction noise can be expected.

Puerto de Mogán

Sometimes known as the "Venice of the Canaries" for its appealing architecture, waterside location and picturesque bridge across the canal-like *barranco*, Puerto de Mogán has more charm than most of the other resorts on this coast put together. What was once a dirt-poor fishing village in a remote part of the island was transformed in the early 1980s by the construction of a **marina**, holiday apartments, shops and restaurants. Low-rise and small-scale, with traffic-free lanes and bougainvillea everywhere, this development has stood the test of time remarkably well. The water in the harbour is astonishingly clear – despite the luxury yachts and motor cruisers that fill it

– and the harbour front is a suntrap, making it an ideal spot for al fresco dining and people watching.

The town is one of the most popular excursions on the island and on Fridays, when the rather tacky tourist **market** (8am–2pm) fills the streets, it is swamped. Recently, the grey **Playa de Mogán** was upgraded into a splendid arc of golden sand, backed by a well-designed new traffic-free promenade which has quickly attracted some high quality restaurants, while inland a new resort suburb is gradually filling the valley floor with large-scale development – the *Cordial Mogán Playa* hotel alone has 950 rooms.

Rather aloof from all this, the old fishing village clings to its cliff, its narrow, stepped streets peaceful and cool, with lots of flowers and skinny cats. There's nothing specific to see here, but it's a pleasant enough area for some aimless strolling.

Mogán

From Puerto de Mogán the main road swings inland and begins its slow, gentle ascent of the lush Barranco de Mogán, passing through several roadside hamlets with exquisite gardens and small-scale plantations of pawpaw, mango and other exotic fruits until it finally reaches Mogán itself, almost at the head of the valley and backed by imposing escarpments. Mogán is a sleepy place, despite being the seat of the local *ayuntamiento* (town hall); there are one or two good places to eat, and the early nineteenth-century church

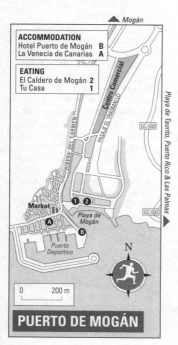

▲ Mogán

ACCOMMODATION
Hotel Puerto de Mogán   **B**
La Venecia de Canarias   **A**

EATING
El Caldero de Mogán   **2**
Tu Casa   **1**

Centro Comercial

PASAJE EL TRASMALLO

RIBERA DEL CARMEN

GC-500

Playa de Taurito, Puerto Rico & Las Palmas

Market

Playa de Mogán

GC-500

Puerto Deportivo

N

0   200 m

PUERTO DE MOGÁN

Yellow Submarine

One of the more unusual excursions from Puerto de Mogán is the journey to the bottom of the Atlantic offered by the Yellow Submarine (Atlántida Submarine SL, Local 389, Puerto de Mogán ☎928 565 108; €27.50), a small but big-windowed modern passenger sub that makes hourly descents from 10am to around 5pm daily. The journey lasts 45 minutes, there are special buses from all along the coast that combine the trip with a visit to Puerto de Mogán itself, and it's worth watching out for special offers.

of St Anthony of Padua contains contains wood engravings that are worth a look if the church is open. Just to the south of Mogán, at **Molino de Viento**, there's a recently-restored windmill at the roadside. There's no entrance charge, but during the day you can usually wander round the interior, though it doesn't quite live up to the beautiful exterior. A short distance beyond the village an unsurfaced road climbs the Ojeda pass to the reservoir of **El Mulato** before linking with a better road that continues to the reservoir of **Cueva de las Niñas** and the centre of the island at Ayacata. The steep ascent of the Ojeda pass itself, however, is only suitable for 4WD vehicles.

Playa de Veneguera

Blissfully remote and one of the few truly dark volcanic beaches on Gran Canaria, the Playa de Veneguera is a favourite with those who like to get away from it all. It lies at the end of a rough, rocky 13-kilometre track suitable only for hikers or 4WD vehicles, signposted from the main Mogán–San Nicolás de Tolentino road through the settlement of Las Casas de Veneguera. The southwest-facing valley is full of fruit plantations and is extremely attractive, while the black sand beach itself is quite broad, and

there's a camping area. The possibility that this, the last major undeveloped beach in the southwest, might be developed as a tourist *urbanizacíon* rallied environmentalists like no other issue in Gran Canaria in the late 1990s. Recognizing its botanical and geological importance, the parliament of the Canaries voted unanimously in 2003 to preserve Veneguera as a nature reserve.

Los Azulejos

Beyond Las Casas de Veneguera the Mogán–San Nicolás de Tolentino road reaches one of the most remarkable geological features on the island. At Los Azulejos – literally, "the tiles"

▲ PUERTO DE MOGÁN

– a rock wall rears up from the roadside, its exposed face stained ice cream shades of yellow, rusty purple or – most startling of all – a coppery green by the minerals in the rock. The lonely grandeur of the rugged mountain scenery here is a real contrast to the bustling coastal resorts, the hillsides carpeted with highly ornamental succulent euphorbias including the cheerful yellow-green *tabaibales* and proud stands of spurge *(cardónales)*, which resemble organ pipes growing out of the hillside. It's a particularly beautiful sight in winter, when small, isolated waterfalls sometimes flow down the mountainsides. On the highest inland peaks, the pine forests of Ojeda fringe the mountaintops.

Hotels

Gloria Palace Amadores
Avda La Cornisa, Puerto Rico ☎928 128 510, @www.hotelgloriapalace. com. Lush gardens with an artificial waterfall, colourful majolica decoration and a clifftop location with wide sea views and plenty of sun make the *Gloria Palace Amadores* stand out among Puerto Rico's hotels. The public areas are generously sized, as are the rooms, which come with limestone tiled floors and pale wood to give a warm but contemporary feel. Like its sister hotel at San Agustín, its spa majors in thalassotherapy treatments using seawater. €124.

Puerto de Mogán
Club de Mar, Puerto de Mogán ☎928 565 066, @www.clubdemar. com. With an enviable position right on the water's edge at the entrance to the Puerto de

Mogán marina, this relatively small hotel has a simple, tasteful, almost yacht-like feel, with summery, rather Mediterranean rooms, tiled floors, majolica bathrooms and lots of wicker. The pool – and some rooms – look directly over the sea. They also have apartments to rent. €92.

Apartments

Apartamentos Blue Star
Avda de la Cornisa 25, Puerto Rico ☎928 560 993, @www.bluestar.es. The hilltop site means plenty of sun and sweeping sea views for most of the apartments at this big, rather stark budget-priced complex. A funicular railway links the various levels to the reception, which is at the top. The functional apartments sleep up to three people and have tiled floors, a kitchenette, living/dining room and one double bedroom. The third person sleeps on a sofabed. There are two pools, but not much in the way of frills or greenery. €29.

Arizona Bungalows
Avda Gran Canaria, Puerto Rico ☎928 560 880, @www.grupoliberty. com. Among the nicer budget choices on the eastern side of Puerto Rico, these apartments are a short walk uphill from the Centro Comercial Puerto Rico and its nightlife and consequently popular with a young crowd. The grounds are very attractive and each apartment has its own bit of bougainvillea and a spacious terrace. The duplex apartments sleep up to five in two separate bedrooms, making them good value if you're travelling with a group. €55.

La Venecia de Canarias

Urbanizacíon Puerto de Mogán, Local 328 ☎928 565 600, ⓦwww. laveneciadecanarias.net. These one- and two-bedroom apartments are right in the marina of Puerto de Mogán – the "Venice of the Canaries", as it styles itself. This is probably still the prettiest tourist development on the island, with something of the feel of a real village and plenty of luxuriant planting to soften the edges. All the apartments have kitchen, phone and TV; some have balconies or terraces. €60.

Riosol Aparthotel

Avda de la Cornisa ☎928 561 258, ⓦwww.riosolaparthotel.com. Occupying a plum, fortress-like position on the corner of the hill overlooking Puerto Rico, the *Riosol* has truly fabulous views down to the beach and sea. Accommodation is a mix of simply furnished one- and two-bedroom apartments with kitchens, and conventional double rooms. There are two pools, squash and tennis courts, a mini golf range, a games and fitness room and Jacuzzi, plus restaurants and a minimarket on site, while the Centro Comercial Europa is only a short walk away. Apartments €66, doubles €60.

Campsites

Camping Guantanamo II

Barranco de Tauro, signposted off the GC-500 road at Playa de Tauro ☎928 562 098, ⓦwww.campingguantanamo. com. Reception open Mon–Sat 2.30– 4.30pm. Recently relocated 1.6km inland from the coast road (where there's a restaurant bearing the same, rather unfortunate name), *Camping Guantanamo II* is one of the few fully fledged campsites on the island, with caravans and mobile homes as well as spaces for tents. It's a sheltered spot, if rather dusty, for now undisturbed though developers are already moving in on the lower reaches of the *barranco*. The gates close from 11.30pm–7am each night. Adult €4.10, tent €3.30–5.50, caravan €4.50, motor caravan €6.20.

Shops

Cerámica Mogán

On the GC-200 at the southern entrance to Mogán ☎617 868 016, ⓦwww.iandodgsonfinearts. co.uk. Mon–Sat 10am–6pm, Sun 10am–2pm. Locally made, hand thrown pottery in a range of styles both traditional and contemporary make a visit to the Cerámica Mogán a pleasurable part of a trip to Mogán. Some of the pottery is unglazed, inspired by the traditional styles of the island; there are also fine art ceramics. Prices are reasonable.

Cafés

La Parada

At the Parada de Taxis, Puerto Rico. Open 24 hours. This unassuming open-fronted, stand-up bar next to the taxi rank in Puerto Rico is open round the clock offering inexpensive tapas, pizzas, sandwiches and ice creams, washed down with coffee, beer or something stronger.

Restaurants

Apolo XI

Plaza de los Poetas 12, Arguineguín ☎928 735 065. Daily 10am–11pm. The name alludes to the space

▲ COFRADÍA DE PESCADORES

superbly fresh, garlicky *alioli* and wonderful warm bread, then scrutinize the daily specials on the blackboard: chickpea stew with chorizo, delicious grilled tuna or chorizo with melting red and green peppers can be some of the options. Round off with juicy fresh melon and papaya, or home-made *flan* (crème caramel), and expect to pay around €15 for lunch.

centre in the hills between Arguineguín and Maspalomas, which tracked the NASA moon probes in the 1960s and 1970s. There's nothing space age about the food here, though; rather, they serve traditional Canarian dishes, from *gofio escaldado* to *estofado* (beef stew), *ropa vieja* or *callos con garbanzas* – tripe with chickpeas – for €5–9.

Balcón Canario

CC Puerto Rico Local 257, Avda Tomás Roca Bosch, Puerto Rico ☎928 561 658 or 928 159 017. A Hispanic island in the otherwise overwhelmingly British- and Irish-oriented CC Puerto Rico, *Balcón Canario* is a reliable choice for good tapas at reasonable prices: expect a blow-out meal here to cost no more than €15 or so; the tuna *croquetas* are particularly filling. The printed menu doesn't tell the whole story – check the whiteboard at the back for specials, or follow the lead of the locals.

Casa Enrique

C/San José, Mogán ☎928 569 542. Daily noon–11pm. This spacious restaurant on the main street in rural Mogán is well worth the trek from the coast for its excellent tapas. Start off with

Cofradía de Pescadores

Avda del Muelle, Arguineguín ☎928 150 963. Daily noon–11pm. This simple concrete structure inside the port complex at Arguineguín has become something of a legend on this coast, and with the fishing boats moored behind the restaurant the freshness of the fish is guaranteed. Go for the catch of the day and look out for local fish such as breca, grilled and served with *papas arrugadas*, salad and a wedge of lemon. The desserts, which make heavy use of *gofio* and *bienmesabe*, are also worth a try. Prices are moderate, mains are around €7.50.

Don Quijote

Apartamentos Portonovo, Puerto Base, Puerto Rico ☎928 560 901. Daily 2.15–10.45pm. With its long, mostly Spanish wine list and interesting menu including partridge and breasts of quail, this restaurant on the fringe of the Puerto Base is among the most authentically Spanish in Puerto Rico. More familiar choices include *albóndigas* (meatballs), *calamares* and cod in marinera sauce and there are also steaks. Expect to pay €10–12 for a main course.

El Caldero de Mogán

Nuevo Paseo Marítimo, Playa de Mogán ☎928 565 367. Open Mon & Wed–Sun 11am–10pm Sitting on the smart new beachfront promenade at Playa de Mogán, *El Caldero* serves vast paellas, tapas-style dishes including *croquetas de morcilla* (blood sausage croquettes) and apple sauce, and well-presented main courses such as hake fillet with crisp skin, served on a bed of caramelized onions with a roast red pepper sauce. Innovative desserts include a hot soup of forest fruits or carpaccio of pineapple marinated in rum with coconut ice-cream. Choose between the sunny terrace facing the sea or the cooler, darker interior. Around €22 for two courses.

Puerto Escala

Puerto Deportivo, Puerto Rico ☎928 560 690. Daily 8am–10.30pm. The location on the outer harbour wall of one of Puerto Rico's two harbours makes this one of the most relaxing spots for a meal in town. It's little more than an open-sided shack, but the pizzas – from €5.50 – are good, the swordfish is excellent and there are a few more exotic items on the menu, including fried whole baby octopus with thyme. They occasionally have live music from a flamenco guitarist too. Pizzas from €5.50.

Tu Casa

Avda de las Artes 18, Playa de Mogán ☎928 565 078. Daily 11am–11pm. *Tu Casa* is a classy conversion of one of the few remaining original buildings along the beachfront of Playa de Mogán. Inside, it's all framed prints, pale walls and high ceilings with beams; outside, it's a sunny place to see and be seen. Kick off with *papas arrugadas* with *mojo* before moving on to fresh fish or paella, shoulder of young lamb or one of the Italian specialities priced around €9.

Bars & clubs

Harley's Café Dancing

Planta 2, CC Puerto Rico. Sun–Thurs 7pm–2.30am, Fri & Sat 7pm–3.30am. Puerto Rico has dozens of bars crammed into the Centro Comercial all competing to have the loudest sound systems, the most tempting drinks promos and the most annoying touts trying to lure you in. Of the big DJ bars *Harley's* is much the slickest, with a brace of Harley Davidson motorcycles for decor and male podium dancers for a gimmick – not surprisingly, it tends to be especially popular with women.

Live entertainment

Chez Funny Boy

Planta 2, CC Puerto Rico. Daily from 9pm, shows start 10.30pm. Free. Tucked into the quieter, more sedate upper part of the Centro Comercial away from the loud DJ bars, *Chez Funny Boy* is Puerto Rico's very own slice of quick-fire drag cabaret, with outrageous costumes, wigs, broad humour and lip-synching to assorted divas. Very tourist-oriented, it's not particularly gay.

The west coast and the Andén Verde

The great rampart of Gran Canaria's west coast is the antithesis of the buzzing tourist regions to the south, and in some ways its antidote, for this part of the island is as unspoiled as its topography is savage. Between the isolated, tomato-growing community of San Nicolás de Tolentino and the picturesque fishing village of Puerto de las Nieves the high mountains of the Cumbre come crashing down in barely four spectacular kilometres from the 1444-metre heights of the Pico de Tamadaba to the ocean. The rocks on this rugged coast are among the oldest on the island, dating from the eruptions fourteen million years ago that created the island. A celebrated but hair-raising coast road – the Andén Verde – runs the length of the coast, and is without doubt the scenic highlight of the round-the-island drive. Not surprisingly given the rough terrain, beaches are few and generally hard to reach, though they're all the more precious for being relatively empty – especially the remote Playa de Güigüí. This is wonderful country too for keen hikers, with charming, secret pastoral landscapes in the *barrancos* of Tasarte and Tasártico, and villages with their own low-key charm – Puerto de las Nieves most of all.

Barranco de Tasártico

From the Mirador of Tasártico on the main Mogán–San Nicolás de Tolentino road, where there's a makeshift café and good views down into the Barranco de la

---

Visiting the west coast

Driving the Andén Verde requires concentration. The road is well surfaced but narrow and twisting, and for most of its length the drops are precipitous. The drive south from San Nicolás de Tolentino is similarly exhilarating and equally tiring. Minor roads in this part of the island are usually narrow, frequently steep and sometimes still unsurfaced, but they are at least usually quiet. Puerto de las Nieves' **tourist office** is at C/Nuestra Señora de las Nieves 1 (Mon–Thurs 9.30am–4.30pm, Fri 9.30am–3.30pm, Sat 9.30am–noon ☎928 554 382, ⊛www. aytoagaete.es) and has information on various taxi tours of the district. There's no longer a tourist office in San Nicolás de Tolentino but limited tourist information including an English-language guide is available from the *ayuntamiento* (C/General Franco 28 ☎928 892 305, ⊛www.la-aldea.com).

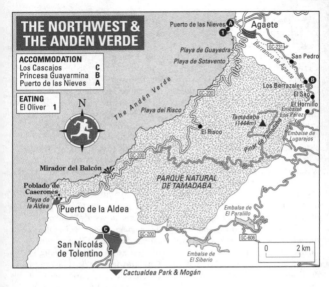

THE NORTHWEST &
THE ANDÉN VERDE

ACCOMMODATION
Los Cascajos   C
Princesa Guayarmina   B
Puerto de las Nieves A

EATING
El Oliver   1

▼ Cactualdea Park & Mogán

Aldea, a narrow minor road – the GC-204 – leads along a rock face into the peaceful little *barranco* of Tasártico. Like many valleys in this part of the island it's a world unto itself, though it's neither as lush nor as large as the *barrancos* of Mogán or Veneguera. After the village of Las Casas Blancas de Tasártico the road through the valley is unsurfaced, continuing to the rocky beach of **Playa de Tasártico**. Long before you reach that, at La Solana, the shorter of the two hikers' routes to the Playa de Güigüí leaves the road on the right. South of the Mirador de Tasártico, in the direction of Veneguera, a minor road leads through the village of Tasarte into the *barranco* of the same name, at the end of which is another pebbly beach, the **Playa de Tasarte**.

Playa de Güigüí hike

The remote, golden sandy beach of Güigüí stands in the heart of a nature reserve, rich in native flora and an important site for seabirds. Güigüí has achieved almost mythical status not just for its beauty – some claim it's the loveliest beach on the island – but because it is just about the most difficult to reach, backed by sheer mountainsides plunging down into the sea. There's no road, so you must either come by sea or on foot across the mountains.

Super Cat excursions departing from Puerto Rico (☎928 735 656) sometimes make it along the coast as far as Güigüí if the weather is fine, but it's not possible to disembark once you get there. Unless you can persuade a fisherman at Puerto de la Aldea to take you, the only option is to walk. There are two **routes**, neither suitable for beginners or the unfit. The longer of the two departs from El Tarajalillo midway between San Nicolás and the coast at La Aldea, and takes five and a half hours, ascending to 700m at the Degollada de Peñon Bermejo and passing the Montaña de los Cedros, the last redoubt of the Canary Island cedar in Gran Canaria. The shorter walk takes two hours from La Solana in the Barranco de Tasártico, and ascends to 650m. For safety reasons don't walk to Güigüí alone, let someone know that you're going, take plenty of water and avoid walking during the hottest part of the day. Most importantly, don't rely on your mobile phone to get you out of trouble, as there are gaps in coverage in this remote part of the island. The English-language **guide** produced by the Ayuntamiento de San Nicolás de Tolentino contains more information and a hikers' map.

San Nicolás de Tolentino

The town of San Nicolás de Tolentino is the biggest settlement in the Barranco de la Aldea, one of the most isolated such valleys on the island. Settlement straggles down the *barranco* all the way from the lush palms of Tocodomán in the south to Puerto de la Aldea on the rocky coast in the north and, for such an isolated spot, it's surprisingly animated, especially

in the town centre where there's a large but rather plain modern church, a few bustling streets and a couple of bars. It's not the most distinguished town on the island architecturally, but there are a few simple old houses in the central traffic-free zone, and a restored windmill at the junction of the Mogán road with the *carretera general* that leads into the town. There's also a small farm museum, the **Museo Vivo** (Cabo Verde, visits by prior arrangement ☎928 890 378) with typical crops and livestock including goats, chickens, cows and a camel. They bake bread and make cheese here too. The town's biggest attraction, however, is **Cactualdea Park** (Carretera de Tocodomán, San Nicolás de Tolentino. Daily: summer 10am–5pm; winter 10am–6pm; €6), a cactus-themed botanical garden with more than 900 varieties of cacti stretching across the hillside south of town on the road to Mogán. Unless there's a bus trip in, it's a peaceful and attractive spot, and if you like what you see the entrance fee gives a reduction on the price of a cactus from the park's own nurseries. There's also a large underground bodega for refreshment. East of San Nicolás de Tolentino, a precipitous but well-surfaced minor road leads past a couple of reservoirs towards the Vega de Acusa plateau and the centre of the island.

Playa de la Aldea

Stoney, steeply shelving Playa de la Aldea is one of the few beaches in this part of the island that has facilities and

▲ CACTUALDEA PARK

▲ PLAYA DE LA ALDEA

is easy to reach. It stretches away from Puerto de la Aldea – Barranco de la Aldea's little port, which has several simple fish restaurants – and has picnic tables under the trees and a promenade. It's also possible to surf here; there's a surfing store, the Aldea Surf Shop, in the centre of San Nicolás de Tolentino (C/Federico Diaz Bertrana 20 ☎928 891 353).

Spanish influence in this part of the island pre-dates the conquest, since monks from Mallorca arrived at Playa de la Aldea as early as 1352. Even earlier, in pre-Hispanic times, the Barranco de la Aldea was the site of an important Canario settlement, the remnants of which, the **Poblado de Caserones**, can be seen a little inland from Puerto de la Aldea, off the Agaete road. There were once between 800 and 1000 homes here.

Mirador del Balcón

High above the ocean, the Mirador del Balcón is a pulpit-like viewing point that rewards a stop with some wonderful panoramas. It's reached by well-made stone steps from the small car park at the side of the GC-200 road, an approach that gives little hint of the truly breathtaking views at the top, extending from the jagged triangular precipices of the Bajones de Ana to the west as far as Puerto de las Nieves to the northeast. There's usually a van selling snacks and drinks in the car park here.

The Andén Verde

From the Mirador del Balcón, the Andén Verde proper starts, a spectacular corniche that is at times hundreds of metres above the sea. The opening of this road in 1939 ended the isolation of the valley of La Aldea and opened up a popular new route for tourists, though locals today would dearly like to see it improved or replaced, as the drive is tortuous. Hugging

The Fiesta del Charco

The Fiesta del Charco (festival of the lagoon) has survived from the times of original Canario culture to the modern day, and remains one of the most popular festivals on the island. It takes place on the Playa de la Aldea at 5pm on September 9 every year, when participants jump into a saltwater lagoon and try to catch fish with their hands. It derives from a native fishing technique known as *embarbascada*, which involved using a latex poison derived from spurges to stun the fish in pools so they could be caught by hand without difficulty.

the contours of the land, the "Green Platform" meanders into steep *barrancos* and around rocky headlands, with the sea far below and the pines of Tamadaba high above. In winter and spring the vegetation is lush and green, with plenty of *cardónales* and *tabaibas* and a few palms at the bottom of the *barrancos*; in summer it is altogether more yellow and dry. After rain the cliff face sometimes glitters with short-lived waterfalls. After 11km you reach the tiny, whitewashed village of **El Risco**, in the *barranco* of the same name, where a roadside bar has drinks and meals, and a dirt track leads down to the **Playa del Risco**, a wide beach of sand and pebbles pounded by the Atlantic surf. A little to the north, just before the Barranco de la Palma, another dirt track - impassable by car – leads down to the even wilder **Playa de Farenoque** a virtually deserted black-sand beach. A few kilometres further on a dirt track leads partway down the Barranco de Guayedra towards another black-sand stretch, the **Playa de Guayedra**. Popular with

locals, it's possible to camp or go diving here, though the sea is rough and there are no facilities. The last 1.7 km to the beach is on foot. The neighbouring **Playa de Sotavento** is rocky, but is a good spot for diving.

Agaete

After the long drive along the Andén Verde the dazzling white village of Agaete appears like some Andalucian mirage. The centre of an agricultural district that has slowly started to sprawl since the GC-2 north coast road was improved, it's an attractive place, though one where it's almost impossible to park in the narrow central streets – the only car park is close to the Huerto de las Flores garden. There were important settlements here before the Spanish came, when the area formed part of the Canario kingdom of Gáldar. A fort was established on the coast nearby during the conquest in 1480, and the current village was founded in 1515. After the conquest, Agaete grew fat on sugar and later on cochineal production and tomatoes. The dominant feature of the town is the high dome of the church

▲ AGAETE

Bajada de la Rama

Like La Aldea, Agaete celebrates an annual festival of pre-Hispanic origin, the Bajada de la Rama – the festival of the tree branch. Every year on August 4 the people of Agaete process down to the sea swinging pine branches taken from the forests of the district. The parade is headed by the *papagüevos* – giant effigies in cardboard representing popular characters of the town, who clear a way through the crowds using their giant hands. The festival has its origins in a rain dance performed by the Canarios.

of **La Concepción**, built in the late nineteenth century and fronting the main square, the Plaza de la Constitución. Next to the square an impressively long stone bridge crosses the usually dry *barranco*, while, just to the east, the **Huerto de las Flores** botanical garden (Mon–Fri 9am–1pm; free) is a lush, if compact, oasis, with many splendid mature specimens of subtropical plants, including flamboyant date palms and bougainvillea.

Puerto de las Nieves

Though it's not quite the sleepy spot it once was, Puerto de las Nieves remains the most perfect fishing village on Gran Canaria, a compact little grid of streets leading down to a harbour and a sheltered pebble and sand beach, from where there are stunning views south along the Andén Verde. It was the port used by the Spanish conquistadors for their assault on the Canario king Guanarteme in his capital of Gáldar. Later, the town profited from the sugar trade with Holland, which is how a famous Flemish triptych, *The Virgin of the Snows*, came to be brought back from Flanders. Thankfully, the town has never quite become an outright resort, retaining the feel of a working port and acting as the departure point for fast ferries linking Gran Canaria to Tenerife. It's also one of the most popular places in Gran Canaria

for a leisurely lunch by the sea – fish restaurants line the beach and harbour.

Puerto de las Nieves' most famous landmark is the **Dedo de Dios** (Finger of God), a slim hand-shaped stack of rock that rises out of the sea a little to the south of the town and which, depending on the light conditions, can be rather hard to make out against the backdrop of cliffs. It lost much of its distinctiveness in a hurricane in December 2005, when the most slender part of the stack broke off during the storm. Almost immediately afterwards, voices were raised in the island's media calling for the rock's pinnacle to be reinstated.

▲ PUERTO DE LAS NIEVES

PLACES The west coast and the Andén Verde

Getting to Tenerife

A pair of fast **ferries** operated by Fred Olsen Express (☎902 100 107, ⌨www.fredolsen.es) maintain a shuttle service between Puerto de las Nieves and Santa Cruz de Tenerife daily from 6.30am to 8.30pm with 8 sailings in each direction, making a day trip to Tenerife feasible, if not particularly cheap. The crossing takes approximately one hour. Return fare for an adult is €61.74; the cost for a car and two passengers is €180.40 return. A free bus to the ferry terminal departs from the Fred Olsen offices at Parque Santa Catalina in Las Palmas one hour before the advertised sailing time.

The tiny **Ermita de las Nieves** is its main architectural monument, a much-restored church that dates back in part to the sixteenth century, though its layout is the result of later rebuilding, and the facade and towers were added in the nineteenth century. The sixteenth-century Flemish altarpiece of the *Virgin of the Snows*, attributed to Joos Van Cleve and for which the church was famous, is now kept at the parochial church in Agaete and is not on public view. Down on the seafront, which seems be constantly undergoing reconstruction, there's a picturesque windmill.

Barranco de Agaete

Despite creeping suburbanization on its lower slopes, the Barranco de Agaete remains one of the most lush and productive valleys on Gran Canaria, its crops including coffee, mangoes, papayas and oranges. Higher up the valley, the hillsides close in around the abandoned former spa of **Los Berrazales**, shuttered and peeling romantically on a superbly scenic site. Immediately above it sits the *Princesa Guayarmina* hotel. The road ends a little over 1km further on at El Sao, from where ancient *caminos reales* (cross-country paths) allow access on foot to the peaceful and picturesquely

situated cave village of **El Hornillo**. Beyond this, paths continue deeper inland into this lovely unspoilt valley landscape, past more cave dwellings and the reservoir of Los Pérez to Lugarejos, where a path crosses the dam across the Embalse de Lugarejos. Keen walkers can ascend to the pine forests of Tamadaba on this path (see p.108).

Hotels

Los Cascajos

C/Los Cascajos 9, San Nicolás de Tolentino ☎928 891 165, ☏928 890 901. In a part of the island where any accommodation – much less budget accommodation – is scarce, the bright, cheerful and reasonably priced *Los Cascajos* is a godsend. The single or double rooms – all with en-suite bathrooms – are simple but clean and comfortable, and the friendly owner also rents out pleasant, sunny one- or two-bed apartments that sleep 3–4. €40

Princesa Guayarmina

Los Berrazales ☎928 898 009, ⌨www.princesaguayarmina.net. This charming, rather old-fashioned hotel stands just up from the now-defunct spa at Los Berrazales, an idyllic spot hemmed in by hills at the top of the lush Barranco de Agaete. The ambience and decor are reminiscent of the 1940s, particularly in the art deco bar. Rooms are big, simple and attractive – not luxurious, but comfortable and airy. Bathrooms are smart and modern. There's a swimming pool, and the hotel offers hydrotherapy, hydro-massage and various beauty treatments too. €60.

Puerto de las Nieves

Avda Alcalde José de Armas, Puerto de las Nieves ☎928 886 256, ⊛www.hotelpuertodelasnieves.net. Bright, modern decor with a nautical theme and several modern artworks in the public areas make this sophisticated little hotel an urbane surprise close to the centre of Puerto de las Nieves. All rooms are soundproofed and have air conditioning, telephone and TV. The ground floor is occupied by a café and à la carte restaurant and the hotel has private parking. There's also a hydrotherapy centre with heated indoor pool, waterfalls, saunas, a gym and a Turkish bath. €96.

Restaurants

El Oliver

Avda de los Poetas, Puerto de las Nieves ☎928 886 179. Daily 10am–8pm *El Oliver* is as good a place as any to savour the quintessential Puerto de las Nieves experience – wonderful fresh fish enjoyed on a simple outdoor terrace with a view of the beach, harbour and the rugged cliffs beyond. They serve superb grilled sardines plus more adventurous fare, including, on Sundays, *sancocho* – a stew of salted fish and potatoes. Prices are reasonable.

The north

From the banana plantations of the coast to the high terraced hillsides of Vega de San Mateo, the north of Gran Canaria is intensively exploited for agriculture and, away from the rocky coast, well watered and lush. This part of the island is densely populated and rich in relics from the pre-Hispanic and colonial eras alike, with impressive archeological sites at La Guancha and the Cueva Pintada, and several lovely historic towns, notably Teror, Santa Maria de Guía and Arucas. There's great natural beauty too, including the awesome natural bowl of the Caldera de Bandama and the precious laurel forests of Moya. The coast here is wild and rocky and popular with surfers, but a few sheltered coves are good for sunbathing and for excellent seafood from beachside restaurants. The north offers plenty of opportunities to sample typical island produce, from the small, sweet Canarian banana to the *queso de flor* cheese of Santa Maria de Guía, the wine of Monte Lentiscal, *gofio* from Firgas and Arucas' celebrated rum.

Sardina del Norte

Brightly-painted luxury homes colonize the clifftops of the west-facing fishing harbour and beach of Sardina del Norte. The smart, well-kept beach is patronized by locals rather than tourists, and is one of the

Getting around and information

From Las Palmas **bus routes** #103 and #105 run the length of the north coast, stopping at Bañaderos and San Andres before serving Santa Maria de Guía and Gáldar; routes #116 and #117 serve Moya. Bus #216 goes to Teror. To reach Arucas and Firgas, take the #204. Other routes spread out from Arucas and Gáldar. The GC-2 coast road is excellent, if congested at times, but elsewhere the roads, while well surfaced, are inevitably twisting due to the steep terrain and are often busy too. The larger towns have **tourist offices**: Gáldar's is in the Casas Consistoriales (Plaza de Santiago 1 ☎928 895 855; July & August Mon–Fri 8am–1.30pm, Sept–June Mon–Fri 8am–2.30pm), and Santa Maria de Guía's in the Casa de la Cultura (C/Canónigo Gordillo 22; Mon–Thurs 8am–3pm, Friday 8am–2pm). Teror's is at Casa de la Huerta 1 (☎928 613 808, ⊛www.teror.es; July–September 9.30am–3.30pm, Oct–June 9.30am–4.30pm) and Moya's at C/Juan Delgado 6 (☎928 612 348, ⊛www.villademoya.com; Mon–Fri 9.30am–12.30pm) In Arucas, it's at Plaza de Constitución 2 (☎928 623 136, ⊛www.arucasturismo.com; Mon–Fri 8am–4pm) and in Firgas at C/El Molino 12 (☎928 616 747; June–Sept Mon–Fri 8am–2pm, Oct–May Mon–Fri 8am–3pm). In Santa Brigida, the office is on the main traffic intersection at C/18 de Julio (⊛www.santabrigida.es; June–Sept Mon–Fri 8am–2pm, Oct–May 8am–3pm).

▲ SARDINA

most popular in the north of the island, partly thanks to its smooth sands and the possibility of windsurfing, sailing and diving, but also because it's a sheltered beach on an often rough coast, and a real suntrap. In addition to the curve of sand, there are rocks and jetties to swim from. The town is also a popular spot to eat fresh fish, and there are several restaurants dotted around the bay. North of Sardina, residential development continues along the coast towards the lighthouse at Punta de Sardina, where the north and west coasts meet.

Playa de Bocabarranco

East of the lighthouse at Punta de Sardina the coast is wild, with swimming in natural rock pools rather than the open sea at El Clavo. Further east, Playa de Bocabarranco is the largest beach in this corner of the island, a broad strip of good sand pounded by rough surf and backed by banana plantations and scrappy-looking houses, though moves are underway to smarten things up with a new promenade. There are also the remains of a few circular stone dwellings dating from pre-Hispanic times just a little way back from the beach across the coast road, and a few more further down the road to Gáldar.

Poblado de El Agujero and La Guancha

The northern coast of Gran Canaria holds one of the most important archeological sites in the whole archipelago, the **Poblado de El Agujero**, a pre-Hispanic settlement, and the settlement's burial ground, **La Guancha** (guided visits only; call ☎928 219 421 ext.4441 for information or enquire at the tourist office in Gáldar). Sitting in the shadow of the Montaña de Gáldar and looking across to Mount Teide on Tenerife – a location that may have had spiritual significance – the site's centrepiece is the Túmolo de La Guancha, the most important pre-Hispanic necropolis in the Canary Islands, a large dry-stone structure built in concentric circles and containing 42 tombs. The complex is fenced off (but visible) between a modern housing development and the sea: the rocky beach of El Agujero in front of it has a seawater pool and is backed by a traffic-free promenade.

Gáldar

Nestling under an ominous but extinct volcano and surrounded by banana plantations, Gáldar was the capital of the *guanartemato* (kingdom) of Gáldar in pre-Hispanic times, and even today remains an important place – much the largest and liveliest town in this area of the island, with a

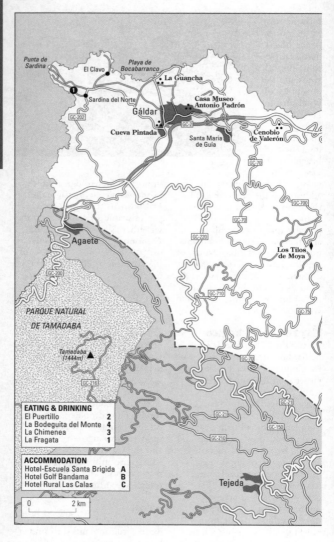

EATING & DRINKING

El Puertillo	2
La Bodeguita del Monte	4
La Chimenea	3
La Fragata	1

ACCOMMODATION

Hotel-Escuela Santa Brígida	A
Hotel Golf Bandama	B
Hotel Rural Las Calas	C

traffic problem matched only by the nightmarish parking. Beyond the jams on the road through the town, however, lies an attractive and historic core, reached along C/Capitán Quesada, the main shopping street. It ends at the Plaza de Santiago, dominated by the church of **Santiago de Gáldar**, unusually large and lofty by Gran Canarian standards, and the first Neoclassical building in the islands. Construction

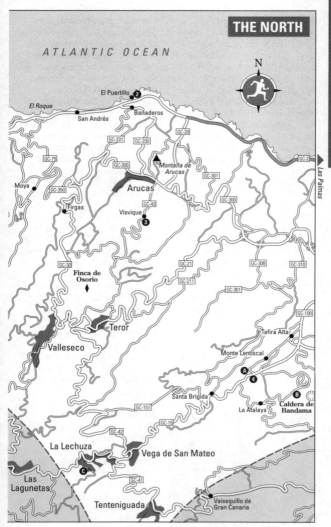

THE NORTH

ATLANTIC OCEAN

N

El Puertillo

El Roque

San Andrés   Bañaderos

GC-20

GC-331   GC-330

GC-75

GC-2

Las Palmas

GC-300

Montaña de Arucas

GC-301

Moya   GC-350

Arucas

GC-300

Firgas

GC-43

Visvique

GC-30

Finca de Osorio

GC-21

GC-308   GC-310

GC-211

GC-361

GC-100

Teror

Tafira Alta

Valleseco

Monte Lentiscal

A

Santa Brígida

La Atalaya

Caldera de Bandama

B

GC-151

La Lechuza

GC-42

GC-15

Las Lagunetas

Vega de San Mateo

C

GC-41

Tenteniguada

Vaisequillo de Gran Canaria

began in 1778 and the church was consecrated in 1826. At the side of the church there's a small museum, the **Museo Arte Sacro** (C/Fernando Guanarteme 2; Tues–Fri 10am–4pm Sat & Sun 10am–1pm; €2), which houses a collection of religious art, including a green baptismal font of Andalucian origin dating from the fifteenth century. Across the square, the lovely nineteenth-century **Casas Consistorales**

156

now houses the tourist office. Its patio is dominated by one of the oldest drago trees on Gran Canaria, with a history documented back as far as 1718. Tucked down C/Tagoror at the side of the Casas Consistorales is Gáldar's imposing **theatre**, which dates from 1912. On the opposite side of the Plaza de Santiago from the Casas Consistorales, and beyond the handsome nineteenth-century casino, a side street leads to the **Casa Museo Antonio Padrón** (C/Drago 2; Mon–Fri 9am–2pm; free) a delightful little art gallery dedicated to the work of Antonio Padrón, an expressionist painter whose work made use of Canarian folk tradition, myths and scenes of everyday life and whose studio this building once was. His woodcuts are gorgeously graphic, and his paintings use the warm colours characteristic of Canarian soil. Gáldar's most important attraction is the **Cueva Pintada** (painted cave; C/Audencia 2 ☎928 895 746, ⓦwww.cuevapintada.org), one of the most significant of Gran

Canaria's pre-Hispanic sites. The complex, discovered in the late nineteenth century, abuts the modern town centre and the paintings here are some of the best surviving examples of Canario art. The cave was excavated by the Canarios from the soft volcanic rock and painted with typically vibrant geometric patterns in red and white. The cave's exact purpose is unclear; various theories suggest it may have been used for funeral rites, as a sacred space or as a dwelling. The Cueva Pintada itself is part of a series of six caves; the wider complex includes sections of the pre-Hispanic town of Agaldar and reconstructions of pre-Hispanic country houses. Unfortunately humidity generated by visitors and damage caused by agricultural irrigation in the district forced the closure of the cave to visitors in 1982. However, after years of patient conservation work and the erection of an impressive new museum, the complex was scheduled to re-open as this book went to press.

Santa Maria de Guía

One of the loveliest colonial towns in Gran Canaria, Santa Maria de Guía is also, appropriately enough, the birthplace of the distinguished Canarian sculptor and architect José Pérez Lujan, known as Lujan Pérez, who was born in 1756. The town's *casco histórico* is dominated by a particularly fine example of his work, the church of **Santa Maria de Guía**. Construction began in 1780 and was completed in 1836, and the church contains examples of his artwork, though it's generally locked except during mass. The centre of the town is

▲ GÁLDAR TREE

▲ SANTA MARIA BALCONY

associated with the banana industry, and the local word *naife* – meaning knife – derives from the English, a reminder of the role British merchants once played in the commercial life of the island. The town's other claim to fame is as the home of *queso de flor*, Gran Canaria's most renowned cheese. Flavoured with the juice of artichokes, it's readily available in local shops and celebrated by a fussily ornamental monument at the foot of C/Médico Estevez.

reached up the steep C/Médico Estevez from the rather grim main road; the entire historic core was declared a national monument in 1982, and it's easy to see why, for there are no eyesores in its pretty, tranquil streets. On the plaza opposite the church the **Espacio Guía** art gallery (C/Marqués de Muni 7, Plaza de Santa Maria de Guía; Thurs–Sat 6–9pm, Sun 11am–2pm; free; ⊛www.insulart. com) is housed in a handsome old house and has interesting, frequently changing exhibitions of contemporary art, often by Canarian artists. At no. 3 Plaza Grande, the seventeenth-century Quintana house has a venerable, sagging, wooden balcony in Canarian Mudéjar style. An enjoyable and well-marked trail – with informative boards in English – leads uphill from the plaza to the little chapel of Ermita San Roque. The houses are painted in all manner of ice cream colours, and the streets are as peaceful as they are beautiful. Santa Maria de Guía was traditionally a centre of knife making, a trade closely

Cenobio de Valerón

GC-291 km 21 Cuesta de Silva, usually Wed–Sun 10am–5pm. About 3km east of Santa Maria de Guía on the old Las Palmas-Gáldar road, high above the coast, the Cenobio de Valerón is perhaps the most visually impressive of all pre-Hispanic sites in the island. A vast fortified communal granary hewn out of the rocky hillside and overshadowed by a massive sheltering rock brow, there are more than 350 caves, chambers, cavities and silos on various levels here, all used for the storage of grain. It was closed for conservation in 2005, but was scheduled to reopen as this book went to press.

Playa de San Felipe

From the strange coastal village of El Roque, which looks like a multicoloured fortress atop its basalt spur jutting out into the Atlantic surf, a road leads along the coast – known here as El Vagabundo – to the single street village of San Felipe, which stands at the mouth of an eponymous *barranco*. The Playa de San Felipe is a surfing hotspot, a broad beach of sand and pebbles on which the Atlantic rollers break dramatically. It's popular at weekends – when it can be difficult to park here – and there are one or two cafés for refreshments.

Moya

Sitting on the rim of a deep, green barranco high above the north coast, Moya is a pleasantly old-fashioned upland town with a main street lined with bars full of old men, and a large, rather self-important modern church, **Nuestra Señora de la Candelaria**, which despite its neo-Canarian architecture dates only from 1957. The site of the church rather than its conservative architecture is the most interesting thing about it, however, as it stands on the edge of a dramatic precipice overlooking the stunning Barranco de Moya. Moya's most famous son is commemorated opposite the church in the **Casa Museo Tomás Morales** (Plaza de Tomás Morales ☎928 620 217, ⊕www.tomasmorales. com; Mon–Fri 9am–8pm, Sat 10am–2pm & 5–8pm, Sun 10am–2pm; free), a likeable small museum dedicated to the modernist poet Tomás Morales, who was born here in 1884. On the ground floor there's a space for temporary exhibitions, but upstairs the museum charts the life of the poet, through paintings, books and artefacts, including some solidly bourgeois nineteenth-century furniture and some racy paintings by José Hurtado de Mendoza. Behind the museum, in C/Léon y Castillo, is Moya's most imposing public building, the Neoclassical **Heredad de Aguas** which, with its clocktower and classical columns, looks a little like a chapel, though it was actually built as the offices of the irrigation association.

Los Tilos de Moya

Just 2.5km southwest of Moya is one of the most important natural sites on the island, the special nature reserve of Los Tilos de Moya. This is one of the last remaining forests of humid laurel or laurasilva anywhere in the world, and the trees look appropriately old and gnarled. The reserve comprises the narrow *barrancos* of Los Tilos and El Laurel, and has, at its entrance, a small Centro de Interpretación (Mon–Fri 9am–1pm; free), behind which a rather pointless show path leads through stands of bamboo a scant 100m or so into the woods. You'll see the laurels far more clearly from the single-track road through the *barranco*, though be warned, it's busy.

Firgas

Best known as the source of the mineral water drunk all over the island, Firgas is, like Moya, a pleasant little upland town, which might barely register on the tourist trail but for the conversion in 1985 of its steeply sloping main street into twin attractions, the **Paseo de Gran Canaria** and the **Paseo Canaria**. The former is a 30-metre long fountain, fringed by flowerbeds and by benches covered in brightly coloured *azulejos* tiles with the framed crests of all the municipalities of the island on the wall behind them. The Paseo Canaria, which is the uphill continuation of the Paseo de Gran Canaria is a series of large-scale relief maps of each of the Canary Islands laid out on the ground in what was formerly the roadway. Around the corner from all this in C/El Molino, next to the tourist office, is the **Molino de**

Gofio or *gofio* mill (Mon–Fri 11am–2pm; free). The water-powered mill was built in 1517 to meet the needs of the local community, and continued in uninterrupted operation until 1959. It was restored and reopened in 1998, and if you ask in the tourist office they'll demonstrate it for you. You can also buy *gofio* made here at the mill. Recrossing the Paseo de Gran Canaria and entering C/18 de Julio, there are fine views down to the coast from between the *ayuntamiento* and the rather simple nineteenth-century church of San Roque. At the end of the street a scenic footpath leads into the Barranco de Azuaje, with views that encompass high meadows and the sheer cliffs far below. A long-distance path follows the *barranco* all the way down to the coast.

Arucas

Surrounded by lush banana plantations and graceful haciendas, Arucas is a handsome old town. Its lovely *casco histórico* has an air of stately repose and is dominated by two great masses of volcanic stone. The larger, the **Montaña de Arucas**, is a volcanic cone, with a road that spirals up to a *mirador*, from where there's a splendid view of Arucas and the north of the island. The smaller of the two masses of stone, the **Iglesia de San Juan Bautista** (Mon–Fri 9.30am–12.30pm & 4.30–5.15pm), sits at the foot of the volcano, its pinnacles soaring like Neogothic space rockets above the surrounding houses of the *casco histórico*. Work started in 1909 to replace an earlier structure dating from 1515 and it was consecrated in 1917 – though work on the bell tower didn't finish until 1977. There's a degree of *modernismo*

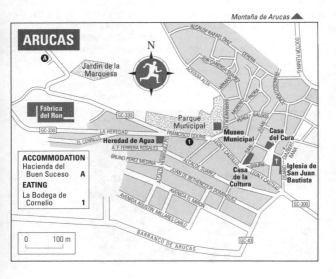

Montaña de Arucas ▲

ARUCAS

Jardín de la Marquesa

Fábrica del Ron

Parque Municipal

Museo Municipal

Casa del Cura

Heredad de Agua

Casa de la Cultura

Iglesia de San Juan Bautista

ACCOMMODATION
Hacienda del Buen Suceso — A

EATING
La Bodega de Cornelio — 1

0   100 m

in the design. The interior is surprisingly restrained, with a forest of pillars flooded with light from the huge rose windows. Diagonally opposite the church door stands the low, whitewashed **Casa del Cura** or priest's house, which dates from the seventeenth century. The church and house face onto the dignified Plaza de San Juan, once the hub of the town but now rather sleepy. From the west door of the church, narrow C/Gourié slices through the town, its tall houses decorated with iron balconies. At its junction with C/Léon y Castillo the local library is housed in the **Casa de la Cultura**, a grand seventeenth-century house with a lovely internal patio that can be seen during opening hours (Mon–Fri 9am–1pm & 4–9pm, July & Aug closes 8pm). Arucas' other main focus is the Plaza de la Constitución, around which are grouped the old town hall, covered market and **Museo Municipal** (Mon–Fri 10am–7.30pm, Sat 10.30am–1pm; free), exhibiting paintings and sculptures by Canarian artists. The museum stands in the **Parque Municipal**, a neatly manicured public park shaded by palms, dracaenas, Canary pines and banana plants. Along the park's southern edge, on

C/Heredad, stands the almost comically dignified **Heredad de Agua** – the headquarters of the local water company – completed in 1912 and topped with a splendid cupola. It's only a few metres' walk from here to the **Fabrica del Ron** (☎928 932 900, ⓦwww.arehucas. com; Mon–Fri 10am–2pm; July & Aug closes 1pm; free), the imposing late nineteenth-century distillery where the island's most famous rum is produced. The factory opened in 1884 to process sugar cane from the island's plantations, but really blossomed in the 1940s when the Arehucas Rum brand was created. The tour takes in an interesting museum, the bottling plant – capable of filling 32,000 bottles an hour – and last, but not least, the tasting room. Below the distillery one of the grandest of the many stately old houses on the GC-330 is the Palacete de la Marquesa de Arucas, a stone mansion dating from 1880 that is the seat of the oldest estate in the Canary Islands. Its garden, the **Jardín de la Marquesa** (Mon–Fri 9am–noon & 2–6pm; €5), contains more than 2500 tropical and subtropical species – including some now extinct elsewhere – and is both decorative and informative, thanks to the booklet you receive for your admission fee. At its centre there's a pool with a topographical map of the island and a very pretty Japanese pavilion.

▲ ARUCAS CATHEDRAL

▲ EL PUERTILLO

El Puertillo and San Andres

The district of Arucas reaches the sea just beyond the *barrio* of **Bañaderos**, where a side turning takes you to the little cove of **El Puertillo** a sheltered bay with a sandy beach, a smart new promenade and a fish restaurant overlooking the beach. Further west, the seafront suburbs of Quintanilla and **San Andres** are strung out along the sea road, which is dotted here and there with huge fish restaurants. The coast here is a surfers' haunt, and the rough Atlantic spray sometimes spatters car windscreens on the coast road.

Teror

It was an apparition of the Virgin Mary atop a pine tree some time during the fifteenth century that turned Teror into a place of pilgrimage and to this day the little town is dominated by the basilica of **Nuestra Señora del Pino** (Plaza Nuestra Señora del Pino; Tues–Fri 9am–1pm & 3–8.30pm, Sat 9am–8.30pm, Sun 7.30am–7.30pm; free, €1.50 to side room). The first, simple chapel on the site was built in 1514, but the poor clay on which it was constructed meant it had to be replaced as early as

1600. The current church was designed in 1760 by Colonel Antonio de la Rocha, who also designed the Hospital de San Martín in Las Palmas. The poor soil has created problems ever since, however, and the church underwent major repairs in the nineteenth and twentieth centuries. Inside, it's unusually ornate for a Canarian church, and there are five altarpieces, dating from 1767–83. The statue of the Virgin of the Pine is displayed in a side room. There's a tradition of dressing the Virgin in gorgeous robes which dates back to 1558; the statue itself was probably brought from Seville at the end of the fifteenth century. Outside, **Plaza del Pino** is the town's main square, and the houses here and in C/Real de la Plaza leading off it have beautiful wooden balconies that contribute strongly to the town's reputation as one of Gran Canaria's prettiest. One of the finest of these houses dates from the seventeenth century and houses the **Patronos de la Virgen** folk museum (Mon–Fri 11am–6pm, Sun 10am–2pm, closed Sat; €3). On the far side of the Plaza del Pino from the basilica is the beautiful **Plaza Teresa de Bolívar**, a garden

▲ NUESTRA SEÑORA DEL PINO, TEROR

square named after the wife of the liberator of the Americas, Simon de Bolívar, a statue of whom adorns the square. The little plaza commemorates Teror's links with the Americas, since Teresa's great-grandfather was born in the town. Behind the basilica, the rather stiff but dignified **Plaza Pio XII** contains the bishop's palace, now a cultural centre. Every Sunday (8am–2pm) the main streets of Teror close to traffic for a very popular **market**, where you can buy food, clothes, arts and crafts. A short distance north of the town on the Arucas road stands the **Finca de Osorio** (☎928 630 090), a wonderful nature education centre standing in extensive grounds that stretch away from the main road towards the Pico de Osorio and which contain woodland and laurel as well as agricultural land. It's only open to organized groups and visits must be booked in advance.

Valleseco

Valleseco or "dry valley" is actually a bit of a misnomer for an area that stands at an altitude of 900m, and is a particularly well-watered spot. Once part of the laurasilva forest of which only a few remnants remain, eighty percent of the district is a protected nature area, reflecting its importance as part of the *monteverde* or evergreen zone. The village itself is fairly diminutive, grouped around a leafy plaza on which stands the church of San Vincente Ferrer, gloomy but rather fine inside, with a simple dome, gothic altar and an eighteenth-century German organ sitting on an elaborately carved balcony. A walking trail follows an ancient *camino real* from Valleseco to Cruz de Tejeda in the centre of the island; along the way it passes the site of one of the island's more recent eruptions, around 3000 years ago.

Vega de San Mateo

With the high mountain ramparts of the island's centre for a backdrop the setting of the town of Vega de San Mateo could hardly be more dramatic. Agricultural terraces scale the slopes above the town almost all

Fiesta of Nuestra Señora del Piño

Teror's liveliest festival and Gran Canaria's largest religious procession takes place in the town on September 7 every year, when each of the island's towns makes offerings of its finest produce to the Virgin of the Pine, the patron saint of the diocese of the Canary Islands whose Saint's Day is September 8. The festivities stretch from mid-August through to late September, and in addition to the religious focus there are football matches and musical performances to keep the festival going.

the way to Cruz de Tejeda, so that despite the savage terrain the signs of cultivation and of civilization are everywhere, in the picturesque houses dotted among the terraces and in the profusion of eucalyptus and pelargonium at the roadside. The town is a fairly low-key place, lacking the polish of the affluent commuter communities around Santa Brígida to the north but with a couple of streets of old houses leading up to the simple parish church. This is wine-growing country, and you may spot the local product on sale in the town's cafés; the area is part of the *denominación de origen* of Gran Canaria. It's also from the district of Vega de San Mateo that the **Barranco de la Mina** water course that eventually leads down to the Guiniguada in Las Palmas starts. The *barranco* got its name (valley of the mine) because water has for centuries been diverted here from the basin of Tejeda. There are remnants of laurel forests and of old water mills, and it's a pleasant place for a walk – the municipality is crossed by ancient *caminos reales*.

Santa Brígida

At Santa Brígida Las Palmas' commuter belt starts in earnest. This is a very affluent corner of the island, as even cursory inspection of the desirable homes lining the main road north all the way down to Tafira Alta demonstrates. Santa Brígida itself is bustling but rather characterless,

with a large chunk of its centre taken over by a new shopping centre and not much in the way of historic architecture. What it does have is the Cabildo de Gran Canaria's **Casa de Vino** (☎928 644 272; Tues–Fri 10am–6pm, Sat & Sun 10am–3pm) in the old Finca el Galéon close to the tourist office – where you can taste local wines – and three bodegas of the **Monte Lentiscal** *denominación de origen* to visit: the Bodega Vandama (Carretera de Bandama 116 ☎639 546 699; Mon–Fri 10am–6pm), the Bodega Mocanal (Carretera de Bandama 68 ☎928 350 970; Mon–Fri 10am–6pm & Sat 10am–3pm) and the Bodega Mondalón (Cuesta Mondalón 8, Los Hoyos ☎928 356 066; by appointment only). Continue along the Bandama road past the wineries and you come to the Real Club de Golf de Las Palmas, the oldest established in Spain, situated on the edge of an extraordinary abyss, the **Caldera de Bandama**. The caldera is an extinct volcanic crater, its volcanic form still quite plain, the upper slopes cliff-like but its floor gentle and green. It's 1km in diameter and 200m deep. A footpath circles the rim of the crater, and another descends to the crater

▲ VALLESECO

The wines of Gran Canaria

The first vines were introduced to the Canary Islands by the Spanish in the fifteenth century, and by the middle of the sixteenth century Malvasia (known in English as Malmsey) and Canaries wines were being exported to northern Europe – Shakespeare made mention of Canary wine more than once. The trade declined through the eighteenth and nineteenth centuries, but in recent years has seen a revival. There are two peculiarities of Canarian wine: first, the island's wide diversity of microclimates means the same grape variety can produce very different results on different sites; and second, the island's vines were introduced before the phylloxera plague that devastated Europe's vines in the nineteenth century so that vines can be cultivated in Gran Canaria without grafting. There are currently two **denominaciónes de origen** on the island, Monte Lentiscal – which covers a compact area around Santa Brigida – and Gran Canaria, which essentially covers the rest of the island, including the bodegas in Vega de San Mateo, Telde and Fataga. Both reds and whites are highly drinkable; chief grape varieties are common black, negramoll, tintilla, white muscatel, malvasia and white listan.

floor, which was once farmed. The northern wall of the crater contains the **Cueva de los Canarios**, a pre-Hispanic grain store. A vertigo-inducing road spirals up the adjacent Pico de Bandama to a car park and *mirador*, which gives impressive views over Las Palmas and the island's northeast. From the golf club, the GC-802 road climbs past opulent villas to the hilltop village of **La Atalaya**, since pre-Hispanic times a centre for pottery production, a tradition continued in the **Centro Locero** (Camino de la Picota 11, La Atalaya ☎928 288 270; Mon–Fri 9am–2pm & 5–9pm, Sat 10am–2pm), signposted off the main street. Here you can see potters using age-old methods and buy the results, with unglazed bowls starting at about €6.

Jardín Canario Viera y Clavijo

On the GC-100 at Tafira Alta. Daily 9am–6pm. ⓦwww.step.es/jardcan. The Jardín Canario, founded in 1952 by the Swedish botanist Eric Sventenius, is laid out across the steep side and wide floor of a *barranco* between Las Palmas and Santa Brigida. This extensive botanical garden contains sections on all the island's major climatic zones and plant types, from the dragon tree walk and laurasilva to Canary pine forest and coastal vegetation. The cacti are particularly stunning, and there are also non-native plants that are nevertheless common in the island, including bottlebrush, frangipan, hibiscus, oleander and bougainvillea. The Jardín Canario is rather badly signposted off the southbound carriageway of the GC-100 –

The World Biosphere Reserve

Gran Canaria was declared a **World Biosphere Reserve** by Unesco in 2005 in recognition of its unusually rich ecosystems. The remoteness of the Canary Islands means that many plants and species survive here that have long since become extinct in more accessible parts of the world. The island also has its own rich store of indigenous plants: more than 100 species are found only on Gran Canaria. That, plus the island's sheer diversity of landscapes and climates means the raw material for a botanical garden is unusually rich.

watch out for the sign directing you to the garden's restaurant. The lower entrance is on the Carretera de Almatriche.

Hotels

Hotel-Escuela Santa Brigida

C/Real de Coello 2, Santa Brigida ☎828 010 414, ⊛www.hecansa. com. Smart business and tourist hotel in lush gardens in Monte Lentiscal, one of the island's smartest residential districts. The ambience is calm and upmarket, and rooms – some with balcony or terrace – are spacious and smart in a conservative modern style. All the features of a business hotel are here – trouser press, Internet access, laundry service, minibar – but with one major difference: the *Hotel-Escuela* is also a school, so that the chefs, waiters, receptionists and other staff tending to your needs are hotel and catering students come to perfect their skills. €84.

Golf Bandama

Lugar de Bandama, Santa Brigida ☎928 351 538, ⊛www.bandamagolf. com. This pleasant hotel, closely associated with Spain's oldest golf club, stands on the rim of what must be the most extraordinary bunker in the world – the 200-metre deep Caldera de Bandama. There's a country club feel to the place; facilities include an open-air pool, tennis courts and a sauna, while the rooms are simple but pretty and most have a balcony or terrace. Some of those facing the caldera don't, but they compensate by having the more spectacular view. €130.

La Hacienda del Buen Suceso

Carretera de Arucas a Bañaderos km

▲ HOTEL-ESCUELA SANTA BRIGIDA

1, Arucas ☎928 622 945, ⊛www. haciendabuensuceso.com. Tucked away on an idyllic banana plantation at the end of a long avenue of bougainvillea, the *Hacienda del Buen Suceso* is a beautiful country house hotel set in the buildings of the oldest estate in the Canary Islands, which dates from 1572. Rooms open onto a stone veranda or galleried balcony, have lofty wooden ceilings, exposed stonework and a stylish blend of modern and traditional decor, including a few canopy beds. The pool juts out into the banana fields, there's a small health suite with hot tub and gym equipment, plus a restaurant and bar and a stylish residents' lounge. €144.

Hotel Rural Las Calas

El Arenal 36, La Lechuza, Vega de San Mateo ☎928 661 436, ⊛www. hotelrurallascalas.com. At this friendly converted country house high in the green hills above Vega de San Mateo the rooms fringe a pretty garden of lavender, white hydrangeas and eucalyptus. In keeping with the rural surroundings, breakfasts in the low, beamy dining room consist of fresh bread, home-made jams and farmhouse cheeses and salamis. The rooms are large and comfortable, decorated in rustic style with very high ceilings and en-suite bath. €86.

Casas rurales

Casa Rural Doña Margarita

C/Padre Cueto 4, Teror ☎928 350 000, ⊛www.margaritacasarural.com. A handsome, late eighteenth-century house in the historic heart of Teror now divided into three, each with bedrooms, bathroom, kitchen and large living/dining room. €70 for two sharing.

Cafés

Tasca La Villa

Plaza Nuestra Señora del Pino 7, Teror ☎928 632 607. Tues–Thurs noon–8pm, Fri & Sat noon–1am, Sun

10am–5pm. Right on the main square in Teror, this smart but informal café-bar serves coffee and cake during the day but also stretches to full meals at around €20 with wine. The *morcilla de Teror* – blood sausage – is a local speciality, served here with glazed onions; otherwise, try prawns *al ajillo*, or the crab and octopus croquettes.

Restaurants

El Puertillo

Paseo Marítimo del Puertillo, Bañaderos ☎928 627 537. Daily 12.30pm–midnight. Perfectly located on the sandy cove of El Puertillo, this restaurant is a good spot to catch the sunset over Tenerife and enjoy excellent fish. The *gofio escaldado* – a fish-stock based soup thickened with *gofio* – is as good as you'll find, the grilled fish is wonderfully fresh and they also do several rice-based dishes. The soundtrack is old-time salsa and the interior is jauntily nautical, but the wide terrace, with its view over the beach and bay, is the place to be. You'll eat well for a little over €20.

La Bodega de Cornelio

C/Francisco Gourie 9, Arucas ☎928 633 485. Weekdays 9am–midnight, Fri & Sat tilll 4 or 5am. A handy little bar opposite the Parque Municipal in Arucas with an outside terrace and a sunny internal patio, *La Bodega de Cornelio* is a good spot for inexpensive tapas, with most dishes €3.50–5. Fill up on tortilla, grilled fish, *pimientos de padrón* and bread with pungent, garlicky *alioli*, washed down with a *jarra* of cool beer.

▲ EL PUERTILLO

La Bodeguita del Monte

Carretera General del Centro, Monte Lentiscal ☎928 430 517 Mon–Thurs 1–4pm & 8pm–midnight, Fri & Sat noon–1am, Sun 1–6pm. Set on a busy restaurant and bar strip in a posh residential district, this buzzy wine bar is a pleasant and informal spot in which to try some of the local wines. Soak up the alcohol with an eclectic selection of dishes including traditional *ropa vieja* stew, bread with *almogrote* – a spicy cheese-based spread – or baby octopus. Prices are reasonable at around €30 for two with wine.

La Chimenea

Carretera General de Arucas a Teror, km 2, Visvique, Arucas ☎928 633 193. Daily except Wed 1–4pm & 8pm–midnight. This bustling steakhouse in an Arucas suburb pulls in an appreciative local crowd for sirloin cooked various ways – with peppercorns, rocquefort, mushrooms, plum sauce or raisins and pine nuts – though they also serve fish dishes and there are Canarian specialities on the menu, including *morcilla de Teror* – blood sausage and superb warm bread with aniseed. Decor is as cheerful as the service with yellow walls and chequered tablecloths.

La Fragata

Puerto de Sardina ☎928 883 296. Tues–Sat noon–5pm & 8pm–midnight, Sun noon–5pm. Big and rather gloomy inside, but with a tiny sunny terrace facing the bay of Sardina, *La Fragata* is the swishest of the seafood restaurants on the Sardina seafront. It's a good spot for a tapas-style lunch – calamares, cheese, salad – or for its more elaborate specialities, which include lobster with rice, baked fish and fish mousse, each around €10.

Restaurant Satautey

Hotel-Escuela Santa Brigida, C/Real de Coello 2, Santa Brigida ☎828 010 414. Mon–Sat 1.30–4pm & 8.30–11pm, Sun 1.30–4pm. The *Santa Brigida* hotel-school's restaurant is in a long, elegant dining room with big French windows fronting the hotel gardens. It's a smart place to enjoy the school's very accomplished cooking, such as deliciously sweet roast peppers and figs with mozzarella, tomatoes and olive oil followed by magret of duck in raspberry sauce or a tender tranche of Iberian pork with oyster mushrooms. Presentation is excellent too and it costs around €25 for two courses.

Essentials

Arrival

Most visitors to Gran Canaria arrive by plane though another option if coming from the Spanish mainland is to take a ferry from Cádiz.

By plane

All passenger flights to the island arrive at the Aeropuerto de Gran Canaria at Gando (☎ 928/579 130, ✆ www.aena.es), just south of Telde on the east coast.

Regular **scheduled flights** by British Airways from London Gatwick cater to non-package visitors and to business travellers, residents and expatriates, while Aer Lingus operates direct flights from Dublin. Most holidaymakers arrive in Gran Canaria on **charter flights** and have a free transfer to their hotel or apartment included in the price of their package. Some tour operators, however, offer lower prices for fewer frills, which may mean making your own way to your resort.

For those getting to their destination on **public transport**, the bus network is a reliable option. To **Las Palmas** bus #60 runs 36 times daily, taking around 20min to Parque San Telmo and a further 15min to Parque Santa Catalina. For **San Agustín**, **Playa del Inglés** and **Maspalomas** bus #66 runs 16 times daily, taking around 30min. Bus #1 serves **Puerto Rico** and **Puerto de Mogán** from the airport, but as it stops only on the

motorway alongside the airport and not in the terminal, it's not suitable for travellers with heavy luggage. Similarly, **Telde** is served by buses #19 and #36 (the latter hourly) and **Aguïmes** and **Ingenio** by the hourly #11 – all of which stop on the *autopista* alongside the airport and not in the terminal. There are no direct buses to the north or west of the island from the airport; take the bus to San Telmo and pick up connections from there. Fares are low: from the airport to Las Palmas costs €1.90; to Maspalomas, €3.30. **Taxis** are a relatively cheap alternative: expect to pay around €20–25 to Las Palmas, €22 to San Agustín, €24 to Playa del Inglés, €30 to Maspalomas, €36 to Arguineguín/Patalavaca, €40 to Puerto Rico, and €49 to Puerto de Mogán.

By ferry

The pricey alternative to flying for those prepared to travel down through Europe first is the ferry from Cádiz, operated by Trasmediterranea (✆ www.trasmediterranea.es). It leaves at 5pm on Saturday and arrives in Las Palmas at 8am on Monday with the return sailing on a Wednesday. The ferry takes cars and accommodation is available in cabins. Meals are included in ticket prices which can be anything upwards of €1400 return for two adults with a car.

Information

The **Cabildo Insular** or Island Council (C/León y Castillo 17, Las Palmas ☎ 928 219 600, ✆ www.grancanaria.com; Mon–Fri 8am–3pm) promotes the whole of Gran Canaria. Its excellent website is available in English and enables you to book accommodation,

research beaches and plan itineraries and activities all over the island. The Internet information is supplemented by free maps and booklets which make use of much of the same information; they're available from the Cabildo Insular and many local tourist offices too. Individual towns have websites of varying quality; those of the municipality of **Mogán** (🌐 www.mogan.es) and of **Maspalomas** (🌐 www.maspalomas. com) are available in English, as is the chief tourist site for Las Palmas, the **Sociedad de Promoción de Las Palmas** (🌐 www.promocionlaspalmas. com) which has interesting sections on the history, architectural monuments and chief tourist attractions of the city. Of generic commercial sites, 🌐 www.gran-canaria-info.com is a useful source of weblinks and 🌐 www.puertorico-tonight. com and 🌐 www.maspalomas-tonight.

com offer useful insights into nightlife in the resorts. Popular British and Irish **newspapers** are widely available in the resorts, either printed in the islands and available the same day or brought in and a day or two old. Of the locally produced English-language publications, the fortnightly **Island Connections** (€1.80; 🌐 www.newscanarias.net) is a local newspaper covering all the Canary Islands while the also-fortnightly and free **Tips & Info** (🌐 www.tipsandinfo.com) is a small-ads based magazine and a mine of information on local services.

Accommodation

There's a great deal of hotel and self-catering accommodation in Gran Canaria but much of it is block-booked by northern European travel agencies, especially in the winter. For independent travellers, many hoteliers and apartment owners do offer the facility to book through their websites, often at competitive rates, though some don't quote these rates publicly to avoid offending corporate customers. This guide only lists hotels and apartments that can be booked independently. Prices quoted are for a high (but not peak) season double room per night, or in the case of self-catering apartments the price to rent the apartment per night. The most useful web portal for this is the Cabildo Insular's Website, 🌐 www.grancanaria. com, which is in several languages including English. Peak season runs from Christmas through to February and again over Easter; the period from May to October is also busy but tends to be cheaper than the winter. In Las Palmas the hotel trade is geared to business travel and prices consequently fluctuate

much less. The capital does have a few hostels aimed at budget travellers, but elsewhere on the island the cheapest option is usually to club together with friends to rent an apartment.

For a more traditonal accommodation option, you can stay in a casa rural or rural house, found in villages or country areas throughout the island, with a concentration in the north and in the Cumbre. Prices depend on the size and standard of fittings, but start as low as €30 per night for two sharing. Local tourist offices have lists or you can contact the Grantural S. Coop Ltda central reservations office in Las Palmas (☎902 157 281, 🌐 www.ecoturismocanarias. com) or, if looking in the north of the island, Gesturgan SCP, C/Principal 49, San Mateo ☎928 661 011.

Camping is not a particularly attractive option; the sheer distance and expense of the ferry trip from Europe makes it expensive for tourers while the dry, stoney ground conditions – especially in the south – are not ideal for tents.

Transport

Getting around Gran Canaria is very straightforward, with a good network of buses serving the main population centres supplemented by cheap, plentiful taxis. Roads are good, with even mountain roads generally well maintained and well surfaced, though frequently twisting and narrow.

Buses

With the exception of Las Palmas, local buses throughout Gran Canaria are operated by Global (🕸 www.globalsu. net), whose distinctive green-blue buses operate a dense and frequent service in the population centres of the north, east and south coasts, and a rather sparser network elsewhere. Fares are low and you can pay on the bus – just tell the driver your destination. Tarjetas de Ida y Vuelta Playa – designed to allow people in the north to travel cheaply to the southern beaches – offer variable discounts on travel at weekends; similar discount cards operate for special events such as Carnival. Timetables are posted at bus stops or available online and in two separate leaflets covering the north and south of the island, available from tourist offices. The bus station or Estación de Guaguas at Parque San Telmo in Las Palmas is the chief hub of the network, and most Gran Canaria towns of any size have their own bus station. Within Las Palmas the yellow buses operated by Guaguas Municipales (☎ 928 446 500, 🕸 www.guaguas.com) offer a cheap and convenient means of getting about the city. The routes have a north-south bias reflecting the shape of the urban area. Tickets cost €0.90 from the driver, or you can buy a Bono Guagua (€5.30) valid for ten trips from the office at San Telmo bus station or from shops including tobacco *estancos*, general stores and newsagents.

Taxis

Taxis are plentiful in Las Palmas and the southern resorts and are usually white with a green light indicating if they are for hire. In town, meters will automatically have €1.35 on them and fares are then calculated at €0.40/kilometre, with supplements at night and during certain holidays. Waiting is charged at €9/hour. Tariffs for inter-urban journeys are €0.42/kilometre with a waiting charge of €11.27/hour and €2.82 for 15min or a fraction of 15min. Rates are higher at night and during holidays, and there's a supplement of €1.65 for journeys on the airport run.

Taxi companies

Costa Canaria Cooperativa de Taxistas de San Agustín ☎ 928 766 767; Cooperativa de Taxistas de Maspalomas ☎ 928 142 634.
Las Palmas Prices Radio Taxi ☎ 928 462 212 or ☎ 928 461 818; Euro Taxi Gran Canaria ☎ 928 460 000; Taxi Radio ☎ 928 465 666.
Puerto Rico and Mogán Cooperativa de Taxistas de Mogán ☎ 928 152 740.
Telde Radio Taxi de San Juan ☎ 928 688 713 or 928 694 908.

Cars

Renting a car is cheap and easy, with dozens of local firms mostly based in the resorts and the major international companies located at the airport and with offices in Las Palmas and the major resorts. Driving – on the right – is generally straightforward; the resorts have wide, modern roads and the highways between towns on the coast are excellent. Getting around Las Palmas by car is stressful and on-street parking difficult and unsafe, though there are good secure car parks. Elsewhere traffic is more moderate and road conditions almost always good, though away from the coast roads are narrower and twisting and driving can be tiring, especially along the few unsurfaced roads that still exist in remote areas and which are only passable using a 4WD vehicle (available from rental outlets). You have to be aged 18–70 and possess a valid driver's licence to rent a car. Day rates for a week-long rental can start as low as €11, though this rises if you're only renting for one or two days. The condition of cars in the resorts is very variable, with popular models such as convertibles or 4WDs often particularly well used, so check the car over before accepting it.

One way to experience the island's scenery without having to drive is on a jeep safari. Discovery Jeep

Safari (☎928 775 188) offers tours of the interior and Doris' Jeep Safari (☎928 784 138) performs the same service specifically for lesbian and gay visitors.

Car rental companies

Airport Auto Reisen ☎928 579 159; Avis ☎928 579 578; Cicar ☎928 579 378; Europcar/Betacar ☎928 574 244; Hertz ☎928 579 577; Moreno Rent a Car ☎901 300 320; Record ☎928 579 347.
Las Palmas Avis ☎928 265 567; Cicar ☎928 277 213; Hertz ☎928 228 846; **Maspalomas** Hertz ☎928 148 179; Moreno ☎928 761 534.
Playa del Inglés Avis ☎928 761 454; Cicar ☎928 767 654; Hertz ☎928 767 054.
Puerto Rico Avis ☎928 561 009; Hertz ☎928 560 012.

Sports & leisure

With settled, fine weather and comfortable temperatures year round, it's not surprising Gran Canaria offers a huge range of outdoor activities on land and sea. Even the least enterprising visitors take advantage of the swimming, fitness or tennis facilities on offer at many hotels or apartment complexes, but for the truly committed the selection is much wider.

Climbing

The rocks and sheer cliffs of the island make it a popular destination for rock climbers. Characteristic landscape features include gullies, cliffs, crests, cauldrons, and rock needles, and there's a complete repertoire of cracks, chimneys, plates, wedges, overhangs and ceilings, making the island basically one immense climbing wall. New and more difficult routes open all the time. Outstanding areas include Roque Nublo, with twelve routes of varying difficulty; El Palmés, in El Toscón de Tejeda, Betancuria in Ayacata or Narices, at the foot of the north face of Roque Bentayga.

Climbing is restricted on this latter rock, because of its archeological value. Close to El Nublo is the rock circus of Ayacata, a sanctuary of traditional climbing with the largest number of classical routes of different lengths and degrees of difficulty. There are also sites in Tamadaba, and at the sea cliff of Bañaderos near Arucas. Sports climbing and boulder climbing takes place in the gullies of the south of the island, including at Sorrueda. With the exception of a few publicly owned places, military sites and sites of ecological sensitivity, climbing is allowed everywhere. Sports climbers do, however, require a federal licence and proper insurance. For more information contact the Federación Canaria de Montañismo (Fedcam; C/Hero 53, Santa Cruz de Tenerife ☻www.fedcam.es).

Cycling

There may not be much pleasure to be gained cycling in the cities or around the resorts, but Gran Canaria's mountainous interior does attract cycling fans and some of the mountain hotels cater specially to cyclists.

Rental companies and tour organizers

Free Motion Avda Alfereces Provisionales, Hotel Sandy Beach Local 9, Playa del Inglés ☎928 777 479, ⊛www.free-motion.net. The biggest bike and outdoor centre in Gran Canaria rents out bikes from around €12 daily, and offers bike tours from €39.50

Happy Biking CC El Nilo, Loc. 155, Avda de Molla, San Fernando ☎928 768 298, ⊛www.happy-biking.com. Bikes from as little as €7.50/day, plus racing and mountain bike tours from beginners upwards.

Diving

There are numerous places off the coast of Gran Canaria for scuba diving, with popular spots including: El Cabrón on the east coast, a marine reserve with rich sealife including barracudas and almaco jacks; Las Palmas, especially the shallows of La Isleta northeast of the port with numerous wrecks; La Baja de Pasito Blanco in the south, a sandy area that is good for underwater photography; and Sardina del Norte, where night dives are possible close to the fishing harbour. Numerous diving schools cater to demand for the sport, most located in the south.

Diving companies

Dive Academy Gran Canaria Club Amigos del Atlantico, C/La Lajilla, Centro Recreativo Puesta del Sol, Arguineguín ☎928 736 196, ⊛www.diveacademy-grancanaria.com. The only diving school on the island with its own private swimming pool offers one day beginners' courses, all PADI courses up to instructor level and diving for all ability levels daily. Prices start from €40 for a snorkelling course, and from €32 for a single dive for a qualified diver.

Diving Center Sun-Sub Hotel Buenaventura, Plaza de Ansite ☎928 778 165, ⊛www.sunsub.com. Daily dives and diving courses from €60 for a resort course, with special courses aimed at children aged 8

and up from €165. Training takes place in the hotel pool and follows PADI and other official training guidelines.

Tortuga C/Churruca 28, Arinaga ☎616 686 439, ⊛www.buceoadaptado.com. A variety of activities adapted for disabled people, from snorkelling to fully equipped dives with a guide.

Fishing

As might be expected for an island far out in the Atlantic Ocean, Gran Canaria offers rich possibilities for sport fishing. Blue and white marlin, swordfish, Atlantic spearfish, tuna and sharks lurk in the waters here, and the richness of the game fishing has led to several records being broken. Biggest choice of boats for rent is in the harbours of the south. Freshwater angling is also possible in the mountain reservoirs.

Fishing companies

Canary Safari Carp Fishing ☎617 977 289, ⊛www.canarysafaricarpfishing.com. Puerto Rico-based British-run outfit offering escorted carp and bass fishing trips to the island's reservoirs, including the Embalse de Chira. Transport from your hotel and all equipment is included in the €80 price.

Sport Fishing Cavalier Puerto Base, Puerto Rico ☎630 189 790, ⊛www.marlincanariasportfishing.com. Daily fishing trips 9am–3pm & 3–8pm, lunch included. Caters to professional and amateur anglers and also for those wanting to spot whales, dolphins, turtles and flying fish.

Golf

Golf has a long history on Gran Canaria and it's not surprising that, given the almost-guaranteed good weather, the island has emerged as a major golf destination. The Real Club de Golf de Las Palmas was the first club in the whole of Spain, founded in 1891, and today has six courses, three close to Las Palmas and the rest in the south of the island, while the golf scene in general is expanding across the island.

Golf clubs

Anfi Golf Barranco del Lechugal, Valle de Tauro, Mogán ☎928 128 840, ✆www.anfitauro.es. Daily 8.30am–6pm.

Campo de Golf de Maspalomas Avda T.O Neckerman, Maspalomas ☎928 762 581, ✆www.maspalomasgolf.net. Daily 7.30am–6.30pm.

El Cortijo Club de Campo Autopista GC-1 km 6.4 Telde ☎928 711 111, ✆www.elcortijo.es. Open to non-members Mon–Fri 8am–12.18pm.

El Cortijo Golf Center Autopista GC-1 km 6.4 Telde ☎928 684 890, ✆www.elcortijogolfcenter.com. Daily 9am–11pm.

Real Club de Golf de Las Palmas Carretera de Bandama, Santa Brígida ☎928 351 050, ✆www.realclubdegolfdelaspalmas.com. Open to non-members Mon–Fri 8am–12.50pm.

Salobre Golf Urbanización Salobre Golf, Autopista GC-1 km 53 Maspalomas ☎928 010 103, ✆www.salobregolfresort.com. Daily 7.30am–7pm.

Sailing

The main areas for sailing around Gran Canaria are the bays of Las Alcaraveneras and Las Canteras in Las Palmas, the east coast, and the resort coasts of the south and southwest. Gran Canaria is something of a powerhouse of competitive sailing, and Gran Canarians form the core of the Spanish Olympic team.

Canary Island lateen sailing is a sub-branch of the sport, in which the disproportionate size of the tall sails relative to the modest dimensions of the hull makes for tricky handling. The season runs from April to October.

Sailing schools

Sailing School Juan Carlos I Federación Insular de Vela, C/Joaquín Blanco Torrent, Las Palmas ☎928 291 567. Boats for hire and instruction available throughout the year, including introductory classes for both adults and children.

Joaquín Blanco Torrent Sailing School C/Olímpico Doreste Molina Puerto Rico ☎928 560 772. Dinghy-sailing tuition for children from ages 8 and up.

Escuela Deportiva Náutica Anfi del Mar Playa Barranco de la Vega, Mogán ☎928 150 798, ext. 1556. Introductory and advanced sailing courses for children and adults.

Club Regatas Suroeste Mogán Playa de las Marañuelas, Arguineguín ☎928 560 772. Sailing and windsurfing tuition for adults and children, both theoretical and practical.

Escuela de Vela Overschmidt Internacional Puerto Escala, Puerto Rico ☎928 565 292. Introductory courses for children and adults, including windsurfing.

Federación de Vela Latina Canaria Esplenada Muelle Deportivo, Las Palmas ☎928 230 616, ✆www.federacionvela-latinacanaria.org. The official body for Canary Island lateen sailing, it has a sailing school which teaches children the techniques of lateen sailing.

Trekking

The stunning landscape and benign climate make Gran Canaria a real paradise for walkers, and the island's 32 protected natural areas are best discovered on foot. There's an intricate network of paths, from easy forest routes and bridle routes to tracks and trails that are strictly for expert hikers and, though short, often very steep. Signposting of the trails is currently being upgraded.

Eurotrekking (☎928 141 187, ✆www.trekkingcanarias.com), offers guided treks through the Canarian countryside each Monday and Thursday, suitable for the inexperienced and mostly lasting a half-day or less.

Surfing and Windsurfing

Gran Canaria's coast offers many opportunities for catching some great waves. In the north, Bocabarranco, San Felipe, Las Canteras (southern end) and La Isleta are all good spots, while Pozo Izquierdo on the east coast is particularly good, and Maspalomas point and the area by the Faro de Maspalomas in the south are both popular too.

This island is considered the world's second best location for windsurfing – only Hawaii beats it – and is home to twelve-times world champion Björn Dunkerbeck, who runs a windsurfing school in the south. Pozo Izquierdo and Vargas on the east coast are world-famous windsurfing beaches.

Windsurfing schools

Centro Internacional de Windsurfing Pozo Izquierdo ☎ 928 121 400, ⓦ www. pozo-ciw.com. Offering accommodation

and a pool as well as its windsurfing school and a school of diving, the centre is located in the windsurfing hotspot of Pozo Izquierdo. Courses start from €80 for children and €100 for adults for ten hours.

Dunkerbeck Windsurfing Center Playa del Aguila San Agustín ☎ 678 893 998, ⓦ www.dunkerbeck-windsurfing.com. This is the school owned by the many-times world champion windsurfer Björn Dunkerbeck. You can rent or buy equipment and it also offers ten-hour beginner courses from €190, and advanced courses starting at €70. They also organisze intensive windsurfing camps, including weekends for children.

Festivals

January 5
Los Tres Reyes Caspar, Beltasar and Melchior – the Three Wise Men – parade through the streets alongside floats featuring children's allegories as part of the Spanish Christmas celebrations. Las Palmas, San Bartolomé de Tirajana and Gáldar are the best places to see these parades.

February
Fiesta del Almendro en flor Folk music and traditional foods are the attractions at this festival in the first fortnight of February, celebrating the blossoming of the almond trees in the upland communities of Valsequillo and Tejeda.

February/March
Carnival Carnival is celebrated with fervour in Gran Canaria, especially in Aguïmes, Las Palmas and Maspalomas. The programme is somewhat loosely related to the liturgical calendar, so that festivities often continue beyond Ash Wednesday into Lent.

March/April
Semana Santa (Holy Week) Processions in Vegueta and Triana, plus concerts of ancient, baroque and sacred music.

April/May
Fiesta del Queso, Santa Maria de

Guía Local farmers invite you to try their products at this annual cheese festival in the island's best-known centre of cheese production, celebrated at the end of April and during the first week of May.

May 30
Dia de las Islas Canarias Canary Island Day is celebrated in Las Palmas with concerts, festivals, sporting events and a firework display.

July
Fiestas del Carmen On the Sundays before and after July 16, the island's fishermen celebrate the festival of Nuestra Señora del Carmen, the patron saint of sailors, by decorating their boats and taking to sea with an image of the Virgin.

July 25
Fiesta de Santiago Apóstol, Gáldar The highlight of this festival honouring the patron saint of Spain is a battle of flowers, but there is a strong cultural side that encompasses folklore, music and art.

August 4
Bajada de la Rama Rain-making festival of pre-Hispanic origin during which the people of Agaete parade down to the sea carrying palm branches and preceded by *papagüevos* – giant effigies of local characters.

August

Fiesta del Agua This water festival at Lomo Magullo, near Telde during the last two weeks in August, ends with water throwing outside the church and attracts a huge following. Perfectly timed to relieve the summer heat, but be warned – tourists are considered fair game.

August 15–29

Virgen de la Cueva, Artenara Each year the Virgin of the Cave is taken from her chapel and carried in procession to the parish church of Artenara, returning to the cave chapel on the last Sunday of the month.

September 7

Fiesta de Nuestra Señora del Pino Gran Canaria's largest religious festival honours the Virgin of the Pine, patron saint of the Canary Islands.

September 9

Fiesta del Charco, Puerto de la Aldea Participants in this strange but extremely popular pre-Hispanic ritual jump into a salt-water lagoon to try to catch fish with their bare hands. It's hugely popular and a bit of a free-for-all so if you manage to get anywhere near the action expect to get wet.

September-October

Virgen del Rosario, Agüimes This festival celebrates water and the island's staple cereal, *gofio*, which participants throw at each other in the streets of the town.

Directory

Addresses Common abbreviations are: C/ for *calle* (street); Ctra for *carretera* (road); Avda for *avenida* (avenue), Edif for *edificio* (building), Aptos for *apartamentos* (apartments) and CC for *centro comercial* (a shopping centre or mall). Within the *centros comerciales* businesses are located by *local* (unit/premises) and *planta* (floor). In towns an address given as C/Gijón 23, 5° means the fifth floor of no. 23 Gijón street. Some addresses use *derecha* and *izquierda* meaning to the right or left of the building; others may have s/n after the street name meaning *sin número* (no number). Outside main towns, addresses are expressed according to the distance from a given point along a road, so that Ctra de Arucas a Bañaderos km 1 means it's on the Arucas-Bañaderos road, 1km from Arucas.

Airlines Aer Lingus ☎902 502 737, ⓦwww.aerlingus.com; Binter Canarias (inter-island flights) ☎902 391 392, ⓦwww.binternet.com; British Airways (operated by GB Airways) ☎928 579 573, ⓦwww.ba.com; ExCel Airways ☎928 579 156 (agent), ⓦwww.xl.com; First Choice Airways ☎928 579 156 (agent), ⓦwww. firstchoice.co.uk; Iberia ☎902 400 500, ⓦwww.Iberia.com; Monarch ☎928 579 156; reservations 800 099 260; ⓦwww. flymonarch.com; Thomas Cook Airlines ☎928 579 585 (agent), ⓦwww.thomas-cook.com; Thomsonfly ☎914 141 481, (agent), ⓦwww.thomsonfly.com.

Banks and exchange The currency in the Canary Islands is the Euro (€). Bank branches, many with ATMs, are plentiful in all the main towns and resorts, and usually open Mon–Fri 8.15/8.30am–2/2.15pm & Sat 8.30am–1pm from October until the end of March, but hours are shorter during Carnival. Some banks open during the late afternoon and evening one day a week and bureaux de change are open longer hours. It is also possible to exchange money in some hotels and in travel agencies, but at less competitive rates.

Consulates British Edificio Cataluña, C/Luis Morote 6, 3°, Las Palmas ☎928 262 508; Ireland C/León y Castillo 195, 1° dcha, Las Palmas ☎928 29 77 28; United States C/Martínez de Escobar 3, 1° oficina 7 ☎928 222 552. Many European and African nations have consulates in Las

Palmas; the nearest representative for most other countries is Madrid.

Customs For customs purposes the Canary Islands do not count as part of the EU. The current limits on what you can import to the UK without paying duty are 2 litres of still wine, 1 litre of spirits or liqueur over 22 percent volume or 2 litres of fortified wine; 200 cigarettes, and 60cc of perfume. You can also bring back £145 of all other goods including gifts and souvenirs.

Emergency services For police, ambulance and fire brigade call ☎112.

Hospitals and clinics Clínica Salus Las Palmeras, CC Kasbah, Avda. de Tenerife 24, Playa del Inglés ☎928 762 992; Clínica Scandinavica, CC Gran Chaparral, Avda. Gran Canaria 30, Playa del Inglés ☎928 771 638; Clínica Scandinavica, Río Piedras 2, Puerto Rico ☎928 725 284; Clínica Scandinavica, Plaza de Canarias, San Agustín ☎928 157 315; Complejo Hospitalario Materno-Insular, Avda. Marítima del Sur, Las Palmas ☎928 444 500; Hospital Clínica Roca, C/Buganvilla 1, San Agustín ☎928 769 004; Hospital de Gran Canaria Dr Negrín C/Barranco de la Ballena, Las Palmas ☎928 450 000.

Internet Internet facilities are most widely available throughout the island in amusement arcades, though there are also a few conventional Internet cafés in Las Palmas. Standards and facilities vary, with some arcades utilizing coin-operated machines and Spanish, rather than qwerty, keyboards. Thirty minutes usually costs around €2.

Mail Post boxes are yellow and marked with a post horn symbol. Stamps (*sellos*) are sold at post offices (*correos*) and anywhere that sells postcards. Post office hours vary but in the bigger towns open from 8.30am–8.30pm weekdays, 9.30am–1/2pm at weekends. In smaller towns it's more typically 8.30am–2.30pm weekdays, and 9.30am–1pm on Saturdays. Deliveries outside the Canaries are quite slow and it usually takes ten days at least for a postcard to reach the UK or mainland Europe (outside Spain).

Pharmacies *Farmacias* are marked with a large green cross and are generally open Mon–Fri 9am–1pm and 4.30–8.30pm, Sat 9am–1pm; a rota of 24-hour duty chemists is posted up outside showing where to go out of hours in an emergency. This information is available online (in Spanish) at ☻www.farmaciascanarias.com.

Telephones Most hotels add surcharges to calls made from their rooms, so it's cheaper to use one of the distinctive blue and green public payphones which require coins, Telefónica phone cards or credit cards. Mobile phones that are compatible with European networks will work in Gran Canaria, but check with your service provider about coverage and call costs. Your phone will not automatically seek out the cheapest local network.

Time Gran Canaria is in the same time zone as the UK and Ireland, making it five hours ahead of the US East Coast and eleven hours behind East Coast Australia.

Tipping In bars and taxis, rounding up to the next euro is fine, while with waiters a 5–10 percent tip is perfectly adequate.

Language

Spanish

Once you get into it, Spanish is the easiest language there is, and you'll be helped everywhere by people who are eager to try and understand even the most faltering attempt. English is spoken in the main tourist areas, but you'll get a far better reception if you try communicating with Canarian Islanders in their own tongue.

For more than a brief introduction to the language, pick up a copy of the *Rough Guide Spanish Dictionary Phrasebook*.

Pronunciation

The rules of **pronunciation** are pretty straightforward and strictly observed.

A somewhere between the A sound of back and that of father.

E as in get.

I as in police.

O as in hot.

U as in rule.

C is spoken like an S before E and I, hard otherwise: *cerca* is pronounced "sairka" (standard Spanish would pronounce it "thairka").

G is a guttural H sound (like the ch in loch) before E or I, a hard G elsewhere – *gigante* becomes "higante".

H is always silent.

J is the same as a guttural G: *jamón* is "hamon".

LL sounds like an English Y: *tortilla* is pronounced "torteeya".

N is as in English unless it has a tilde (accent) over it, when it becomes NY: *mañana* sounds like "manyana".

QU is pronounced like an English K.

R is rolled, RR doubly so.

V sounds more like B, *vino* becoming "beano".

X has an S sound before consonants, normal X before vowels.

Z is the same as a soft C, so *cerveza* becomes "thairbaitha"

Words and phrases

Basics

Yes, No, OK	Sí, No, Vale
Please, Thank you	Por favor, Gracias
Where?, When?	¿Dónde?, ¿Cuando?
What?, How much?	¿Qué?, ¿Cuánto?
Here, There	Aquí, Allí
This, That	Esto, Eso
Now, Later	Ahora, Más tarde
Open, Closed	Abierto/a, Cerrado/a
With, Without	Con, Sin
Good, Bad	Buen(o)/a, Mal(o)/a
Big, Small	Gran(de), Pequeño/a
Cheap, Expensive	Barato, Caro
Hot, Cold	Caliente, Frío
More, Less	Más, Menos
Today, Tomorrow	Hoy, Mañana
Yesterday	Ayer
The bill	La cuenta

Greetings and responses

Hello, Goodbye	Hola, Adiós
Good morning	Buenos días
Good afternoon/night	Buenas tardes/ noches

See you later	Hasta luego
Sorry	Lo siento/disculpe
Excuse me	Con permiso/perdón
How are you?	¿Como está (usted)?
I (don't) understand	(No) Entiendo
Not at all/You're welcome	De nada
Do you speak English?	¿Habla (usted) inglés?
I (don't) speak Spanish	(No) Hablo español
My name is . . .	Me llamo. . .
What's your name?	¿Como se llama usted?
I am English/ Scottish/ Welsh/ Australian/ Canadian/ American/ Irish/ a New Zealander	Soy inglés(a)/ escocés(a)/ galés(a)/ australiano(a)/ canadiense(a)/ americano(a)/ irlandés(a)/ Nueva Zelandes(a)

Hotels, transport and directions

I want	Quiero
I'd like	Quisiera
Do you know. . .?	¿Sabe . . .?
I don't know	No sé
There is (is there)?	(¿)Hay(?)
Give me (one like that)	Deme (uno así)
Do you have. . .?	¿Tiene . . .?
the time	la hora
a room	una habitación
with two beds/ double bed	con dos camas/ cama matrimonial
with shower/bath	con ducha/baño
It's for one person	Es para una persona
For one night	para una noche
For one week	para una semana
How do I get to. . .?	¿Por donde se va a . . .?
Left, right, straight on	Izquierda, derecha, todo recto
Where is. . .?	¿Dónde está . . .?
the bus station	la estación de guaguas
the nearest bank	el banco mas cercano
the post office	el correos/la oficina de correos

the toilet	el baño
Where does the bus to . . . leave from?	De dónde sale la guagua para. . .?
I'd like a (return) ticket to . . .	Quisiera un billete (de ida y vuelta) para. . .
What time does it leave?	¿A qué hora sale?

Numbers and days

1	un/uno/una
2	dos
3	tres
4	cuatro
5	cinco
6	seis
7	siete
8	ocho
9	nueve
10	diez
11	once
12	doce
13	trece
14	catorce
15	quince
16	diez y seis
17	diez y siete
18	diez y ocho
19	diez y nueve
20	veinte
21	veintiuno
30	treinta
40	cuarenta
50	cincuenta
60	sesenta
70	setenta
80	ochenta
90	noventa
100	cien(to)
101	ciento uno
200	doscientos
500	quinientos
1000	mil
Monday	lunes
Tuesday	martes
Wednesday	miércoles
Thursday	jueves
Friday	viernes
Saturday	sábado
Sunday	domingo
today	hoy
yesterday	ayer
tomorrow	mañana

Food and drink

aceitunas	olives
agua	water
ahumados	smoked fish
al ajillo	with olive oil and garlic
a la marinera	seafood cooked with garlic, onions and white wine
a la parilla	charcoal-grilled
a la plancha	grilled on a hot plate
a la romana	fried in batter
albóndigas	meatballs
almejas	clams
almogrote	a paste of goat's cheese, tomato, chilli and garlic, often served as an appetizer.
anchoas	anchovies
arroz	rice
asado	roast
bacalao	cod
berenjena	aubergine/eggplant
bienmesabe	literally "tastes good to me" – a blend of almonds and honey used widely in desserts
bocadillo	bread roll sandwich
boquerones	small, anchovy-like fish, usually served in vinegar
cabra	goat
café (con leche)	(white) coffee
calamares (a la romana)	squid (fried in batter)
cangrejo	crab
cebolla	onion
cervéza	beer
champiñones	mushrooms
chorizo	spicy sausage
churros	doughnut-like batter strips served for breakfast with thick hot chocolate
conejo	rabbit
crema catalana	Spanish version of crème brulée
croquetas	croquettes, usually with bits of ham in
cuba libre	rum and coke
cuchara	spoon
cuchillo	knife
empanada	slices of fish/meat pie
ensalada	salad
ensaladilla	russian salad (diced vegetables in mayonnaise, often with tuna)
flan	creme caramel
fresa	strawberry
gambas	prawns
gofio	finely ground mix of wheat, barley or maize, usually accompanying soups and stews
gofio escaldado	a thick, soup-like dish based on fish stock and gofio, often on menus as a starter but hearty enough for a light lunch
huevos	eggs
jamón serrano	cured ham
jamón de york	regular ham
langostinos	langoustines
leche	milk
lechuga	lettuce
manzana	apple
media ración	large plate of tapas (literally "half portion")
mejillones	mussels
mojo	garlic dressing available in rojo (spicy "red" version) and "verde" ("green", made with coriander)
morcilla	black pudding/blood sausage
naranja	orange
ostras	oysters
pan	bread
papas arrugadas	unpeeled new potatoes, boiled dry in salted water

papas alioli	potatoes in garlic mayonnaise
papas bravas	fried potatoes in a spicy tomato sauce
pimientos	peppers
pimientos de padrón	small peppers, with the odd hot one
piña	pineapple
pisto	assortment of cooked vegetables, similar to ratatouille
plátano	banana
pollo	chicken
pulpo	octopus
pulpo a la Gallega	octopus served sliced with olive oil and paprika
queso	cheese
ropa vieja	literally "old clothes", a stew of meat with chickpeas and vegetables
salchicha	sausage
setas	oyster mushrooms
solomillo	sirloin steak
sopa	soup
té	tea
tenedor	fork
tomate	tomato
tortilla española	potato omelette
tortilla francesa	plain omelette
vino (blanco/ rosado/ tinto)	(white/rosé/red) wine
zarzuela	Canarian fish stew
zumo	juice

Glossary

almogarén place of pre-Hispanic religious rituals, generally on an elevated site
avenida avenue
ayuntamiento town hall
barranco gorge
barrio suburb or neighbourhood
bodega wine cellar; can also be a restaurant
calle (usually abbreviated to C/) street or road
camino real high road; ancient cross-country track or path
casco histórico historic core (of town)
CC (centro comercial) shopping and entertainment mall

edificio building
ermita hermitage or chapel
hacienda large manor house
guagua local name for buses
iglesia church
menú del dia daily menu in a restaurant
mercado market
mirador view point
Mudéjar Spanish-Moorish architecture
parador state-run hotel, usually housed in buildings of historic interest
playa beach
plaza square
terraza outdoor bar/club

Travel store

For more information go to www.roughguides.com

Stay In Touch!

Subscribe to Rough Guides' **FREE** newsletter

News, travel issues, music reviews, readers' letters and the latest dispatches from authors on the road. If you would like to receive roughnews, please send us your name and address

UK and Rest of World: Rough Guides, 80 Strand, London, WC2R 0RL, UK
North America: Rough Guides, 4th Floor, 345 Hudson St,
New York NY10014, USA
or email: newslettersubs@roughguides.co.uk

www.roughguides.com

Information on over 25,000 destinations around the world

- **Read** Rough Guides' trusted travel info

- **Access** exclusive articles from Rough Guides authors

- **Update** yourself on new books, maps, CDs and other products

- **Enter** our competitions and win travel prizes

- **Share** ideas, journals, photos & travel advice with other users

- **Earn** points every time you contribute to the Rough Guide
  community and get rewards

Listen Up!

Rough Guide Music Titles

Bob Dylan • The Beatles • Classical Music
Elvis • Frank Sinatra • Heavy Metal • Hip-Hop
iPods, iTunes & music online • Jazz
Book of Playlists • Opera • Pink Floyd • Punk
Reggae • Rock • The Rolling Stones
Soul and R&B • World Music Vol 1 & 2

BROADEN YOUR HORIZONS

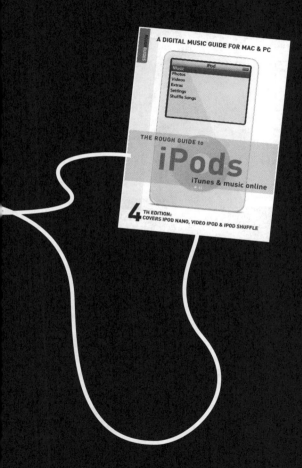

"Brilliant! ... the unmatched leader in its field"

Sunday Times, London, reviewing The Rough Guide to the Internet

A DIGITAL MUSIC GUIDE FOR MAC & PC

iPod

Music
Photos
Videos
Extras
Settings
Shuffle Songs

THE ROUGH GUIDE to

iPods

iTunes & music online

4 TH EDITION:
COVERS IPOD NANO, VIDEO IPOD & IPOD SHUFFLE

BROADEN YOUR HORIZONS

ROUGH
GUIDES

THE ROUGH GUIDE to
chick flicks

Samantha Coo

THE ROUGH GUIDE BOO

Playl

500 irresistible playlist ideas f

2nd Edition

A DIGITAL MUSIC GUIDE FOR MAC & PC

THE ROUGH GUIDE to
iPods
iTunes & music online

4 TH EDITION:
COVERS IPOD NANO, VIDEO IPOD & IPOD SHUFFLE

12 Editions • 3 Mi

THE ROUGH GUIDE to
ebaY

Ian Peel

THE ROUGH GUID

The
Inte

The filth • the fury • the fashion

HE ROUGH GUIDE to
Punk

Al Spicer

The songs • the singers • the stories • the soul

THE ROUGH GUIDE to
Soul and R&B

Peter Shap

THE
THE N
THE T

THE ROUGH GUIDE to
THE DA VINCI
COD

Michael Haag and Veronica Haag

Navigate the blogosphere

THE ROUGH GUIDE to
Blogging

Jonathan Yan

lained

a

THE ROUGH GUIDE to
Pink Floy

small print & Index

A Rough Guide to Rough Guides

In 1981, Mark Ellingham, a recent graduate in English from Bristol University, was travelling in Greece on a tiny budget and couldn't find the right guidebook. With a group of friends he wrote his own guide, combining a contemporary, journalistic style with a practical approach to travellers' needs. That first Rough Guide was a student scheme that became a publishing phenomenon. Today, Rough Guides include recommendations from shoestring to luxury and cover hundreds of destinations around the globe, including almost every country in the Americas and Europe, more than half of Africa and most of Asia and Australasia. Millions of readers relish Rough Guides' wit and inquisitiveness as much as their enthusiastic, critical approach and value-for-money ethos. The guides' ever-growing team of authors and photographers is spread all over the world.

In the early 1990s, Rough Guides branched out of travel, with the publication of Rough Guides to World Music, Classical Music and the Internet. All three have become benchmark titles in their fields, spearheading the publication of a range of more than 350 titles under the Rough Guide name, including phrasebooks, waterproof maps, music guides from Opera to Heavy Metal, reference works as diverse as Conspiracy Theories and Shakespeare, and popular culture books from iPods to Poker. Rough Guides also produce a series of more than 120 World Music CDs in partnership with World Music Network.

Visit www.roughguides.com to see our latest publications.

Rough Guide travel images are available for commercial licensing at www.roughguidespictures.com

Publishing information

This 1st edition published September 2006 by Rough Guides Ltd, 80 Strand, London WC2R 0RL. 345 Hudson St, 4th Floor, New York, NY 10014, USA.

Distributed by the Penguin Group
Penguin Books Ltd, 80 Strand, London WC2R 0RL
Penguin Group (USA), 375 Hudson Street, NY 10014, USA
14 Local Shopping Centre, Panchsheel Park, New Delhi 110017, India
Penguin Group (Australia), 250 Camberwell Road, Camberwell, Victoria 3124, Australia
Penguin Group (Canada), 10 Alcorn Avenue, Toronto, ON M4V 1E4, Canada
Penguin Group (New Zealand), Cnr Rosedale and Airborne Roads, Albany, Auckland, New Zealand
Cover concept designed by Peter Dyer
Typeset in Bembo and Helvetica to an original design by Henry Iles.

Printed and bound in China
© Neville Walker 2006

No part of this book may be reproduced in any form without permission from the publisher except for the quotation of brief passages in reviews.
208pp includes index

A catalogue record for this book is available from the British Library

ISBN 1-84353-533-5

The publishers and authors have done their best to ensure the accuracy and currency of all the information in Gran Canaria DIRECTIONS, however, they can accept no responsibility for any loss, injury, or inconvenience sustained by any traveller as a result of information or advice contained in the guide.

1   3   5   7   9   8   6   4   2

Help us update

We've gone to a lot of effort to ensure that the first edition of Gran Canaria DIRECTIONS is accurate and up-to-date. However, things change – places get "discovered", opening hours are notoriously fickle, restaurants and rooms raise prices or lower standards. If you feel we've got it wrong or left something out, we'd like to know, and if you can remember the address, the price, the phone number, so much the better.

We'll credit all contributions, and send a copy of the next edition (or any other DIRECTIONS guide or Rough Guide if you prefer) for the best letters. Everyone who writes to us and isn't already a subscriber will receive a copy of our full-colour thrice-yearly newsletter. Please mark letters: "Gran Canaria DIRECTIONS Update" and send to: Rough Guides, 80 Strand, London WC2R 0RL, or Rough Guides, 4th Floor, 345 Hudson St, New York, NY 10014. Or send an email to mail@roughguides.com

Have your questions answered and tell others about your trip at www.roughguides.atinfopop.com

Rough Guide credits

Text editor: Clifton Wilkinson
Layout: Diana Jarvis
Photography: Neville Walker, Eddie Gerald
Cartography: Katie Lloyd-Jones
Picture editor: Mark Thomas

Proofreader: Serena Stephenson
Production: Katherine Owers
Cover design: Diana Jarvis

SMALL PRINT

The author

Neville Walker first visited Gran Canaria on a cheap deal in 1993, and has been back to the island almost every year since, writing articles about it for newspapers and magazines in the UK, USA, Ireland and South Africa. He has worked on the Rough Guides to London, Austria, France, and Provence & the Côte d'Azur. This is his first complete book for Rough Guides.

Acknowledgements

The author would like to thank everyone who made researching and writing this book easier. Thanks to Alma Perez at the Spanish Tourist Office in London, to Magui at Hotel Rural Las Calas, Peggy Betancor Bravo de Laguna, Paula Schlueter at the Cabildo Insular, Federico Espino-Martel and Michael Duignan, to Dave at the diving school in Arguineguín, and to Raymond at Respect in Playa del Inglés. Thanks above all to Geoff Howard and my editor Clifton Wilkinson at Rough Guides in London and to Geoff Hinchley, Isobel and Kathryn Walker.

Index

Maps are marked in colour

INDEX